in Portuguese

The all-in-one language and travel guide

Peter Bull

Matthew Hancock

BBC Books

Developed by BBC Languages
Series adviser: Derek Utley
Edited by Virginia Catmur
Audio producer: John Green, tefl tapes
Concept design by Carroll Associates
Typeset and designed by Book Creation Services, London

Cover design by Carroll Associates
Cover photo: Robert Harding Picture Library

ISBN 0 563 40053 6

Published by BBC Books, a division of BBC Worldwide Ltd
First published 1998

Printed and bound in Great Britain by Cambus Litho, East Kilbride
Colour separations by DOT Gradations, Chelmsford

Photographs
All photographs copyright Michelle Chaplow, except:

A.G.E. Fotostock: back (b)
The Image Bank p27(b)
Life File p27(m), p29
Pictor International – London p26, 28(b)
Roland Oliveira p90(b)

INTRODUCTION

Get By in Portuguese will enable you to pick up the language, travel with confidence and experience the very best the country has to offer. You can use it both *before* a trip, to pick up the basics of the language and to plan your itinerary, and *during* your trip, as a phrasebook and as a source of practical information in all the key travel situations.

Contents
Insider's guide to Portuguese An introduction to the country a guide to the main cities and region-by-region highlights for planning itineraries.
Bare necessities The absolute essentials of Portuguese.
Seven main chapters covering key travel situations from *Getting around* to *Entertainment and leisure*. Each chapter has three main sections: *information* to help you understand the local way of doing things; *Phrasemaker*, a phrasebook of key words and phrases; *Language works / Try it out*, simple dialogues and activities to help you remember the language.
Menu reader A key to menus in Portuguese.
Language builder A simple introduction to Portuguese grammar
1000-word dictionary The most important Portuguese words you will come across with their English translations.
Sounds Portuguese A clear guide to pronouncing the language

How to use the book
Before you go You can use the *Insider's guide* to get a flavour of the country and plan where you want to go. To pick up the language, the *Phrasemaker* sections give you the key words and phrases; the *Language works* dialogues show the language in action and *Try it out* offers you a chance to practise for yourself.

During your trip The *Insider's guide* offers tips on the best things to see and do in the main cities. The *Phrasemaker* works as a phrasebook with all the key language to help you get what you want. Within each chapter there is also practical 'survival' information to help you get around and understand the country.

ortugal's historical setting

For such a small country, Portugal is geographically diverse and boasts a rich cultural heritage. Although it is now one of Western Europe's poorer states, the Portuguese built up an empire between 1419 and 1750 which covered almost alf the globe's coastal trading areas; the wealth accumulated uring these times is still evident in the churches, monasteries and ansions of today.

Portugal retained much of its empire until the 1970s, when it elinquished control of countries that it no longer had the power to fluence. In 1974, a revolution deposed the repressive regime of the ctator Salazar, which had made Portugal an isolated and backward ountry. After this revolution, residents of the former colonies were lowed to settle in Portugal, so that today larger Portuguese towns ave sizeable communities from Africa, Macau and Goa, cultures hich have influenced Portugal's food and music. There are also

many Brazilians in Portugal; until recent European Union regulations took effect, Brazilians did not need a visa to live or work in the country. Since 1974, the country has seen enormous economic growth, partly aided by European Union funds, although its inland rural areas retain a traditional agricultural lifestyle.

Like Spain, Portugal has a Catholic tradition, was occupied by Moors and had a sea-based empire, but there are few other similarities between these Iberian countries. The

Portuguese language looks similar to Spanish when written, but it sounds utterly different.

Although Portugal is proud of its independence from Spain, which it has been at war with in the past, nowadays new trade links are being forged with its former foe and Portugal remains strongly in favour of the European Union.

The Portuguese people, geography and climate

The Portuguese people are a gentle and reserved race, perhaps the legacy of a distant Celtic influence. Once you get talking, you will find most Portuguese extremely courteous and friendly, prepared to go out of their way to help visitors.

Portugal faces the Atlantic, the ocean which allowed Portuguese explorers to open up global trade, and which also gives it a level of rainfall nearer that of northern European countries. Combined with its warm climate, the result is a unique and surprising lushness, and what is more, nearly all the rain falls in the winter months, especially November and March.

■ **The north of Portugal,** from the commercial city of Oporto to the Spanish border in the east, can get rain all year, while the mountainous

interior can be bitterly cold in the winter. Nevertheless, the people are perhaps the friendliest in Portugal. The beaches of the Costa Verde have a wild appeal in summer, while the dramatic mountains and twisting river valleys of the Minho and Trás os-Montes are some of the most beautiful areas of the country, ideal for walking from spring to autumn.

■ Best visited from May to October, **central Portugal** contains some of the country's most interesting towns such as the university centres of Évora and Coimbra, the pilgrimage city of Fátima and historic Tomar. Lisbon is one of Europe's most beautifully situated capital cities, while the coastline consists of a series of sandy if wave-battered beaches. The mountainous interior is most attractive in the Serra da Estrela mountain range, ideal for hiking or even, in winter, for skiing.

■ **The south of the country** is the driest area and remains mild even in winter, while summers can be scorching. Natives of the Alentejo are a friendly people who work in a harsh region stretching across kilometres of flat agricultural land. This is a region of white-washed towns and olive groves, while the coastline is craggy and relatively undeveloped. The Algarve is famous as being the best area for warm sea and great beaches. Though the coast gets crowded here, the rolling inland Algarve offers picturesque solitude.

Currency/Changing money

change money or traveller's cheques in travel agents, hotels and banks on presentation of your passport. Banks open from 8.30 am to 3 pm from Monday to Friday, but be warned that commission for currency or traveller's cheques can be extortionate. Larger resorts also have automatic exchange machines which can exchange foreign notes.

The Portuguese currency is the *escudo*, which is divided into *centavos* although these are worth so little that you will rarely see them. It is written: 2$50 (2 *escudos* and 50 *centavos*), 250$00 (250 *escudos*) etc. You will also hear the word *contos*, colloquial for thousands of *escudos*, as in 25 *contos* (25,000 *escudos*).

Portugal is inexpensive by European standards. Most hotels, larger shops and supermarkets will accept major credit cards. For cash, your best bet is to withdraw money from automatic cash machines which are to be found in nearly all towns of any size. These accept most major credit cards and you only pay a minimal fee for the transaction. Failing this, you can

Visas and entry requirements

You do not need a visa if you are from Australia, New Zealand or are a member of the European Community, and indeed at many of Portugal's border crossings with Spain passports are rarely checked. Technically you are allowed to stay for 90 days before you need to apply for an extension at the nearest District Police headquarters.

American and Canadian nationals also do not need a visa and are entitled to stay for 60 days. South African nationals can obtain a visa from their nearest Portuguese embassy or consulate, valid for between ten and 30 days. For addresses of embassies and consulates in Portugal, see p100.

Lisbon

*L*isbon rarely disappoints the first-time visitor, even though it has fewer historical sites than many European capitals. Its main appeal lies in just wandering round and soaking up the atmosphere. Set on steep hills overlooking the wide Tagus estuary, its aspect is often compared to San Francisco, a feeling compounded by its street trams and suspension bridge. Its atmosphere, however, is closer to South America than the States, the city made up of gracefully decaying buildings and a series of noble squares, interspersed with modern developments and decrepit shanty towns. The visitor will find most of interest around the Baixa (the lower town), an area built after the great earthquake of 1755. This stretches from the breezy riverfront Praça do Comércio to the bustling Rossio. Also of interest are the Bairro Alto (the upper town) and the Alfama, which clusters round the slopes of the castle and predates the times of Moorish occupation. In contrast, Lisbon's futuristic Expo 98 site is a redeveloped area with a hi-tech Ocean Pavilion, one of Europe's largest oceanaria.

Don't miss

A ride on tram route 28, which rattles its way through the Baixa and up the steep gradients of the Alfama.

A walk round the castle walls of the ruined Moorish Castelo de São Jorge with its panoramic views of the city.

A wander round the Alfama through its network of tiny, steep streets and stairways: getting lost amongst the white-washed buildings is half the fun.

A trip to Belém, a riverside suburb which is home to the Manueline Mosteiro dos Jerónimos and the Torre de Belém, monuments to the great Portuguese discoverers.

A visit to the Fundação Calouste Gulbenkian, containing a modern art gallery and a wealth of art from around the world; don't miss the Egyptian room and the Lalique jewellery collection.

A look in Alfama's churches of São Vicente de Fora – where most of Portugal's kings are laid to rest – and the domed Santa Engrácia, which affords views over the twice-weekly flea market, Feira da Ladra, and the river beyond.

Shopping in the Baixa, a grid of mainly pedestrianized streets full of traditional and art deco shops.

A ferry ride over the Tagus from the arcaded Praça do Comércio to the fishing port of Cacilhas for a different perspective of the city.

A ride up the steep slopes to the Bairro Alto on one of two funicular railways (*elevadores*) or in the eccentric, lift-like Elevador Santa Justa.

A visit to the Bairro Alto's landmarks, to see the ornate interior of the church of São Roque, and the ruined gothic Convento do Carmo.

A night out on the town in the Bairro Alto or on the riverfront, both full of bars, restaurants and clubs offering *fado* (Portugal's traditional folk music), live music or the latest dance sounds.

Clubs and bars

Adega do Ribatejo (Rua do Diário de Notícias 23, in the Bairro Alto) A good place to eat and listen to live *fado*.

Frágil (Rua da Atalaia 126) An exclusive nightclub for the trendy and young in a great building in the Bairro Alto.

Hot Clube de Portugal (Praça da Alegria) A tiny basement club which hosts some big jazz stars.

Instituto do Vinho do Porto (Rua de São Pedro de Alcântara 45) A limitless selection of ports is served in this somewhat formal bar in the Bairro Alto.

Kremlin (Escadinhas da Praia 5) Another fashionable nightclub near Santos station, which gets going at around 2 am.

Pavilhão Chinês (Rua Dom Pedro V 89) An eccentric bar in the Bairro Alto, stuffed full of collector's items and with a long cocktail list.

Ritz Clube (Rua da Glória 57) A huge old club with a dance hall usually vibrant with live African music.

Pé Sujo (Largo de São Martinho 6–7) An intimate club with catchy, live Brazilian bands.

Try a coffee and pastry in

Pastelaria Suiça (Praça Dom Pedro IV 96) Outdoor tables overlook the Rossio and the spacious Praça da Figueira.

Café Nicolá (Praça Dom Pedro IV 26) A tiny traditional café on the Rossio.

A Brasileira (Rua Garrett 120) A famous intellectuals' drinking hole in the fashionable Chiado shopping district.

Antiga Confeitaria de Belém, (Rua de Belém, Belém) Serves up the tastiest *pastéis de nata* (custard tarts) in Portugal.

Have a meal in

Bota Alta (Travessa da Queimada 37) A characterful and always popular Bairro Alto restaurant serving generous portions of Portuguese dishes.

Casa Faz Frio (Rua Dom Pedro V 96) A very traditional, small restaurant at the top end of the Bairro Alto.

Cervejaria Portugália (Avenida Almirante Reis 117) Good for cheap seafood; always lively until the small hours.

Cervejaria da Trindade (Rua Nova da Trindade 20) A beautifully tiled restaurant in the Bairro Alto, although better for quantity than quality.

Gargalhada (Costa do Castelo 1) An Alfama restaurant which adjoins a circus school, with superb food and even better views over Lisbon.

Martinho da Arcada (Praça do Comércio 3) A smart traditional restaurant, famous for its associations with the poet, Fernando Pessoa.

Solmar (Rua das Portas de Santo Antão 108) One of a row of quality seafood restaurants in the Baixa.

Tégide (Largo Academia das Belas Artes 18) A grand, up-market restaurant with a great outlook, serving quality Portuguese dishes.

Tertúlia do Tejo (Doca de Santo Amaro) Classy Portuguese cuisine in one of Lisbon's liveliest night spots, under the suspension bridge.

Children's Lisbon

Lisbon, like Portugal in general, is child-friendly and children of all ages will be welcomed in virtually any bar, café or restaurant. Children will enjoy many of the 'Don't miss' activities listed above; plus the Feira Popular, by Entrecampos metro, a summer fairground in Lisbon with fun rides for children.

Note the Fundação Gulbenkian has its own childcare facilities for four- to twelve-year-olds. There are many open spaces for children in Lisbon, but be careful of fast-moving traffic on major roads.

Useful metro stops:

- **São Sebastião** for the Gulbenkian museum.
- **Restauradores** for the *elevador* to the Bairro Alto.
- **Rossio** for the Praça da Figueira and the Baixa.
- **Socorro** for the 12 or 28 tram to the Alfama.
- **Saldanha** for the main bus station.
- **Campo Pequeno** for the bull-ring.
- **Colégio Militar** for the Estádio da Luz, said to be the largest football stadium in Europe, and home to Benfica.

Trams and funiculars

Trams are a fun if slow way to get around central Lisbon, although there is a fast new tram line to Belém. The tram company, *Carris*, also run Lisbon's *elevadores* (funiculars), the short railways and lifts which help avoid a sweaty climb up Lisbon's steeper hills.

Lisbon's transport

City buses

Lisbon has a good bus system. Bus routes and fare zones are displayed on bus stops (see p41). Remember that Lisbon has a traffic problem; avoid travelling during the rush hours (8–9 am and 4–6 pm).

Train routes to local sites

- Cais do Sodré to Cascais, via Santos, Belém and Estoril.
- Rossio to Sintra and Queluz.

The metro

In Lisbon, the metro is gradually being extended to Cais do Sodré and the Expo site. Metro tickets are cheaper in blocks of ten than individually: buy them at the station ticket office, or from the automatic ticket machines above the platforms. The metro runs from 6 am to 1 am.

Ferries

MONSA
LX-3146-

Sintra

Ferries run from around 6 am to midnight. Car ferries leave from Cais do Sodré. Useful crossings include:
■ From Praça do Comércio or Cais do Sodré to Cacilhas, where there are buses to Caparica and Sesimbra.
■ From Praça do Comércio to Barreiro station for trains south.

Daytrips from Lisbon

Sintra–Cabo da Roca–Queluz
Sintra is the former summer hilltop retreat for the Portuguese royals and aristocracy; don't miss the fairy-tale Pena palace or the views from the ruined Moorish castle. With a car, go on to Cabo da Roca, a rocky

Cabo de Roca

headland which is the most western part of mainland Europe; or by train, you can return to Lisbon via Queluz palace, a former royal residence with lovely gardens.

Cascais–Guincho–Estoril
Cascais is a fashionable coastal resort with some traditional Portuguese mansions. By car or bus, go on up the coast to Guincho, with its wild sandy beach that hosts international surfing competitions; or by train, you can return to Lisbon via Estoril, another coastal resort famous for its casino.

Mafra
Mafra is a small town with a massive 18th-century convent. Don't miss its vast library, royal apartments and a room completely furnished in antlers and animal hides.

Sesimbra–Parque Natural da Arrábida
Sesimbra is a pretty coastal town with a fine beach. Getting there is half the fun; take the ferry over the Tagus for connecting buses in Cacilhas, or take a bus over the vertiginous Ponte 25 de Abril suspension bridge. With a car, go on to the Parque Natural da Arrábida. This mountainous nature reserve has some calm sandy bays for swimming, while muscatel grapes are grown on the slopes.

Oporto

*C*entral Oporto is a fascinating place, its vibrant commercial areas and bustling shops and cafés contrasting with the riverside where much of historic Oporto is crammed densely on the north bank. The steep narrow alleys of this part exude an almost Dickensian atmosphere. The ancient streets become an extension of the tightly-packed houses, with children playing football on the steep cobbles and people chatting or barbecuing sardines on the doorsteps of their homes. There is no longer a major port on the Douro here, but the riverfront is the area for restaurants, bars and nightlife, while over the double-tiered Ponte Dom Luís bridge lies Vila Nova de Gaia, home to the port wine trade.

Don't miss

A boat trip up the Douro, a one-hour ride from Vila Nova de Gaia which passes under all four of Oporto's bridges, offering a relaxing taster of Oporto's atmosphere.

A trip to the port wine lodges in Vila Nova de Gaia. The various companies all offer tours round their lodges, many of which date back to the early 1700s. The big names like Sandeman and the smaller family-run companies like Calem all offer free tastings.

A stroll along Cais da Ribeira, the atmospheric riverfront which children use as a diving board for swims in the river. Buy fruit from the small market by the bridge or stop for a drink in the lively Praça da Ribeira.

The Bolsa and the church of São Francisco, two of Oporto's most ornate buildings. The Bolsa is the Stock Exchange and its interior shows the wealth created by Portugal's nineteenth-century traders.

A climb up the Torre dos Clérigos, a church tower which offers superb views over Oporto's terracotta-tiled rooftops.

A ride on tram route 18, Oporto's last surviving central tram, a great way to see Oporto from Rua do Carmo to the mouth of the Douro.

A stroll from São Bento to the Ponte Dom Luís. Look out for the ornate decorative *azulejo* tiles in São Bento station; walk onto the dizzy top tier of Ponte Dom Luís for a great perspective of the city.

A walk from the Sé to the riverfront. Wander round the Sé, Oporto's chunky cathedral, then wend your way steeply down through the tightly-knit cobbled alleys to the riverfront; on Saturdays, you will find the lively flea market below the Sé.

A visit to the Museu Nacional Soares dos Reis, a museum with a collection of Portuguese art, sculptures, ceramics and glass in an impressive former palace.

Have a drink or a meal in

Aquário Marisqueiro (Rua Rodrigues Sampaio 163) One of the best places to have seafood, near the town hall.

A Brasileira (Rua do Bonjardim 118) An art deco building with a restaurant and café area north of São Bento.

Casa Filha da Mãe Preta (Cais da Ribeira 39) One of the more up-market riverside restaurants; go to the tiny upstairs room for views over the Douro.

Café Guarny (Avenida dos Aliados) A big airy café, the perfect place for a breakfast croissant or a light lunch and particularly popular for tea.

Lunchtime cafés, which serve ridiculously cheap and wholesome three-course set lunches to local workers, with prices usually including wine; try any in Rua da Vitória, south of the Torre dos Clérigos.

Café Majestic (Rua de Santa Catarina 112) A smart art deco café with outdoor tables, aπ perfect coffee-stop in one of Oporto's best shopping streets.

Solar do Vinho do Porto (Rua Entre Quintas) The place to have port, with an outdoor terrace just beyond the Jardim do Palácio de Cristal.

Taverna do Bébobos (Cais da Ribeira 24) A fine old restaurant on the riverfront with great fish dishes.

Taverna Filha da Mãe Preta (Rua Canestreiros 26) For a very cheap glass of wine amongst the locals, round the back of – and a complete contrast to – the restaurant of the same name.

Vila Nova de Gaia riverfront cafés; some serving drinks from giant port barrels, all offering great views over Oporto and the *barcos rabelos*, the sailing barges traditionally used to transport the port wine.

Children's Oporto

Children are generally welcomed in all cafés and restaurants. The Jardim do Palácio de Cristal has a Quaker animal hospital in the grounds of its spacious park; children may also enjoy the bird market, held on Sunday mornings behind São Bento station. In May, ask in the tourist office for details of Oporto's puppet festival.

Oporto's transport

If you don't mind climbing hills, you can walk to most of Oporto's sites. Taxis are relatively cheap; otherwise, use the extensive bus network or tram 18 (see p10).

Useful routes:

■ **To the airport** from Jardim da Cordaria: bus 56, roughly 30 minutes.

■ **To the port lodges** from Avenida dos Aliados: buses 82/83/84.

■ **For trains south,** go from São Bento and change at Campanhã.

■ **For trains north and east,** go direct from São Bento, except for the line to Póvoa de Varzim which leaves from Trindade.

Daytrips from Oporto

Amarante The train from Oporto to Amarante (two hours) takes twice as long as the bus, but is one of the most picturesque train rides in Portugal. Amarante itself is a pretty town on the river Tâmega, with lovely old houses overlooking the water.

■ Take a pedalo ride on the gentle river.

tomb of São Gonçalo

■ Visit the church by the bridge to see the tomb of São Gonçalo, worn almost smooth by the touch of those seeking marriage from his saintly powers.

■ Don't miss the Cubist works of Amadeo de Sousa Cardoso in the museum which has taken his name.

Vila do Conde A small resort, the old centre being slightly inland. It's the nearest town to the north of Oporto and worth visiting for its clean beaches.

■ Have a drink on Praça da República and watch the activity of the fishing port on the river Ave.

■ Visit the Convento de Santa Clara, a hilltop convent connected to an impressive ruined aqueduct.

■ Follow the river down to Guia and Forno beaches, where the sea is sheltered by an ancient fort, for excellent swimming.

Póvoa de Varzim A large and brash resort, which is always lively:

■ Enjoy the huge – but usually crowded – expanse of sandy beach.

■ Visit the casino.

■ Enjoy the bars and discos such as Sector 7 and Hotel Ver o Mar on the seafront.

Espinho Just south of Oporto, this is not the prettiest resort in Portugal, but has a good beach, a casino, a golf course and fine nightlife.

Northern Portugal

Northern Portugal has less sunshine than the rest of Portugal, but this is more than compensated for, as the area has some of the country's most spectacular landscapes. The Costa Verde has a long, sandy stretch of coastline, while inland there are picturesque river valleys from the gently winding Lima to the dramatic contours of the Douro and Tâmega. Towards the eastern Spanish border, the countryside becomes wild and mountainous, with fantastic walking territory in the Peneda Gerês national park and the rural stretches of Trás-os-Montes.

Don't miss

Great beaches: the Costa Verde

This northerly stretch of coastline is not for those who like balmy sea water, but the beaches tend to be quieter than elsewhere. Some of the best beaches include:

Vila Praia de Âncora A popular summer destination for Portuguese, overlooked by two small forts. The town is nothing special, but swimming is good from the long beach or in the sheltered river estuary, while evenings see the whole town out on the promenade.

Afife A tiny place which boasts a casino to lure people the one and a half miles from its fantastic sandy beach.

Viana do Castelo The main Costa Verde resort, with a neat historic centre lying on the river Lima.

■ Have a drink in the pedestrianized Praça da República, with its fountain, 16th-century almshouses and impressive town hall.

■ Take the funicular to the hilltop basilica on Monte de Santa Luzia for a fantastic view of the coast.

■ Take a ferry over the Lima to Praia do Cabedelo, a crescent-shaped beach for sand, windsurfing and refreshing swims.

■ Walk down the Jardim Marginal along the riverfront, a cool garden shaded by scented lime trees.

■ Visit Viana's rambling Friday market, near the old castle.

Historic towns and sights

Guimarães One of Portugal's oldest and most beautiful towns.

■ Don't miss a drink stop in Praça de Santiago or Largo de Oliveira, two squares in the heart of the medieval centre.

■ Visit the castle, birthplace of Afonso Henriques, founder of the Portuguese nation.

■ See the ancient stone monument, the Colossus of Pedralva, in the Museum of Martins Sarmento.

■ Take a ride on the Teleférico da Penha, a high-tech cable-car, or take a bus to the lofty heights of Penha Santa Marinha da Costa monastery.

Braga Portugal's religious capital and one of the north's largest and liveliest cities.

■ Don't miss the Sé, one of Portugal's oldest buildings; inside this eleventh-century cathedral, visit the Capela dos Reis where the parents of the founder of Portugal are laid to rest.

■ Have a coffee in Café Astória, a traditional coffee house overlooking the expansive main square, Praça da República.

■ Take a bus or taxi or drive the two and a half miles to Bom Jesus do Monte, a church at the top of a spectacular stairway; don't miss the leafy gardens and boating lake behind the church.

Braga cathedral

itânia de Briteiros These mospheric remains show the esence of a large 2000-year- d Celtic settlement and are erhaps Portugal's most impressive cavations. The foundations of ats, a cistern, paved streets and d town walls can be reached from raga and Guimarães.

aldas do Gerês This is a small ghteenth-century spa town, deep in e heart of the mountainous scenery the Peneda-Gerês national park. eer into the spa building where ater gushes out at 45°C, ideal for aring respiratory ailments. Drive up the wooded valley to ortela do Homen, the border post ith Spain, on a Roman route once lled Military Road 18; look out for e Roman pillars marking distances. op off for a swim in one of the reams set amongst the pine-trees. Walk up to the Pedra Bela *iradouro*, a viewpoint with a ectacular outlook. Continue to e Arado waterfalls where you n swim in the deeper pools.

ragança, a historic town in the far orth-east of Portugal.

■ Don't miss the medieval walled town. Climb the keep for a great view over the surrounding countryside, and look at the nearby granite pig, a prehistoric fertility symbol.
■ Visit the museum of Abade de Baçal, displaying medieval stonework, sacred art and traditional clothing in a former bishop's palace.
■ Have lunch or dinner in Solar Bragançeno, a lovely traditional manor house which has been converted into an up-market restaurant.

Tours of the main sights of the north

Route 1
This tour from Oporto takes in a combination of market towns, resorts and impressive fortified towns (car/train).
■ Stop in Barcelos, a historic riverside market town, famed for its enormous weekly market (see p59).
■ Continue to Viana do Castelo, the Costa Verde's liveliest resort (see p14).
■ Visit Caminha: once an important port, this is an attractive town at the mouth of the river Minho with a lovely town square. It is just a short walk from some great beaches.

■ Hop off in Vila Nova de Cerveira: this small town has a lively art college and you can see innovative modern art on display amongst the town's historic buildings. Stay in the castle, now a *pousada* (up-market hotel), or take the ferry over the Minho to swim from the river beach in Spain.

■ Stay in Valença: the end of the rail line has an impressive walled town enclosed by huge fortifications built to protect it from Spain on the opposite side of the river. Nowadays it is a great place to buy souvenirs or to have dinner. Don't miss its weekly market (see p59).

Route 2

A circular route up the Minho into the national park of Peneda-Gerês, taking in graceful towns, traditional rural villages and some of Portugal's wildest scenery (car).

■ From Valença (see above) continue up the river Minho valley, terraced with vineyards for *vinho verde*, the distinctive light young wine

■ Have lunch in Monção, an attractive town with a reputation for gastronomic excellence. Don't miss the local river trout, or some Alvarinho wine, one of the best *vinhos verdes*.

■ Continue via the pretty spa town of Penso to Melgaço: you can glimpse the deep Minho valley from the walls of its ruined castle.

■ Climb the twisting road into the Parque Nacional de Peneda-Gerês, through some of Portugal's craggiest scenery. Look out for herds of wild Garrano horses.

■ Stop at the mountainside village of Peneda, with the spectacular steps leading to its holy church, the destination of a Catholic pilgrimage on 7 September.

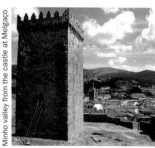

Minho valley from the castle at Melgaço

Wend your way down the dirt road to Soajo and Lindoso, two traditional mountain villages with stone houses and curious, tomb-like granite grain-stores.

Head west out of the park through the attractive market towns of Ponte da Barca and Ponte de Lima. Have a meal in the latter overlooking its ancient stone bridge. In either town, try the fantastic local *vinho verde* or take a walk over the river Lima to be among the verdant vineyards.

From Ponte de Lima, it is easy to return to Valença, or to go on to Viana do Castelo or Oporto.

Route 3

A circular route up through Trás-os-Montes (car).

At Vila Real, don't miss the Mateus palace, one of Portugal's most impressive country houses with a beautiful ornate garden. Take a return ride on the single-track rail route from Vila Real to Régua (see p39).

Detour to the traditional stone houses in the Parque Natural do Alvão. Go on to the spa town of Vidago and have a drink or lunch in the amazingly grand Hotel Palácio. Stop over in Chaves, a pleasant functional border town with

traditional wooden-balconied houses; take a pedalo ride down by the Roman bridge. Sample the local *presunto* smoked ham, and climb the town's castle keep to look over the terracotta rooftops.

■ Take the beautiful mountain road to Bragança (see p15) via Vinhais and the wild beauty of the Parque Natural de Montesinho, great for walking or picnicking.

■ Take the winding old road back to Vila Real or the fast IP4 road if you have less time.

Route 4

This route takes you deep into Trás-os-Montes, right up to Portugal's border with Spain, through fortified frontier towns and over the terraced slopes by the river Douro where port wine is grown.

■ From Bragança, take the beautiful winding road to Miranda do Douro, once the religious capital of the region and still a picturesque walled town set on the Douro above a deep gorge.

■ Continue to Mogadouro, a provincial town with an impressive castle, famed for its steaks. Drive on to Torre de Moncorvo, an ancient town set in some of Portugal's wildest mountains.

■ Drive down a road which comes alive with almond blossom in February, to Vila Flor. Don't miss its amazing museum, a wacky collection of local goods ranging from the town's first telephone to ancient typewriters.

■ Cross the Douro valley at the railhead town, Pocinho, and go on to Vila Nova de Foz Côa. Take a jeep safari to a gorge containing possibly the largest concentration of Palaeolithic art in Europe.

■ For a leisurely return to Oporto, take the twisting N222 back along the Douro valley via Régua, or continue:

■ Stop off in Trancoso, a small but perfectly preserved walled town and former Jewish stronghold. From here it is easy to pick up a fast road back to Oporto via Viseu.

port vineyards at Régua

Mirando do Douro

Central Portugal

*T*his large area, easily accessible from Lisbon, offers a diverse range of attractions from fine walking country to historic towns and lesser known coastal resorts.

Don't miss

Great beaches and resorts

Figueira da Foz The main resort on a great stretch of coastline running all the way from Aveiro. Figueira has a wide beach, a casino, surfing and lively old streets packed with restaurants.

Pinhal de Leiria This sandy coastline is backed by an ancient pine forest, with several small resorts near the historic town of Leiria.

Nazaré Set below steep cliffs, Nazaré is a large and lively resort which tourists share with fishing folk who still wear traditional costume.

São Martinho do Porto Set in a sheltered natural circular bay, this attractive small resort offers safe swimming for children.

Ericeira Just north of Lisbon, Ericeira is famed for its lobsters and is a favourite haunt for weekenders from Lisbon, up for its beaches and nightlife.

Larger towns not to be missed

Coimbra This ancient town was once Portugal's capital and now is best known for its university.
■ Visit the Velha Universidade; don't miss the Chapel's *azulejo* tiles or the eighteenth-century library.
■ Look in the museum of Machado de Castro, displaying furniture and sculptures in the beautiful palace of a former archbishop.
■ Have a coffee in Café Santa Clara, built into part of a monastery with outdoor tables overlooking Coimbra's best shopping streets.

Coimbra university

■ Explore the Portugal dos Pequeninos, a park full of replicas of Portugal's great buildings, interesting for adults and fun for children to squeeze in and out of the models.

■ Go to Conímbriga, half an hour south-west of Coimbra, the site of a Roman town where you can still see Roman roads, mosaics, an aqueduct and pools. Don't miss the museum with details of the excavations.

Conímbriga

Tomar This small town in the Ribatejo region is famous for being the home of the Knights Templar, medieval knights who were loyal to the Pope.

■ Explore the expansive Convento de Cristo, the twelfth-century knights' headquarters.

■ Inside, don't miss the Charola (knights on horseback are said to have prayed in front of this temple) or the amazing Manueline windows of the Chapter House.

■ Take a drink by the Ponte Velha in the old town overlooking the river Nabão.

pillars of the Temple of Diana, Évora

Évora A UNESCO heritage site, Évora is a beautifully preserved university town in the Alentejo district.

■ Don't miss the pillars of the Roman temple in the heart of Évora.

■ Walk along Rua do Cano and follow the course of the ancient aqueduct through the old town.

■ Have a drink in Praça do Giraldo, the impressive main square full of students and men in traditional Alentejan capes.

■ Look in the church of São Francisco, with its bizarre Chapel of Bones, lined with the skulls and bone of monks.

■ Stroll into the courtyard of the old university, decorated with *azulejo* tiles.

Tours of the main sights of Central Portugal

Route 1

This route takes you into Serra da Estrela, one of Portugal's most beautiful national parks and perfect hiking country.

■ From Coimbra, drive on to Luso, a spa town on the edge of some beautiful walks in the Buçaco forest. Have a swim in Luso or take tea in the elegant *salão do chá* tea house.

■ Head inland to Guarda, one of Portugal's highest towns; don't miss the sturdy cathedral in its arcaded main square.

■ Enter the Serra da Estrela natural park via the town of Covilhã. Go up to the winter skiing centre of Penhas da Saúde, the start of some great walking country around Torre, Portugal's highest mountain.

■ Don't miss the traditional Serra da Estrela mountain villages of Manteigas, Sabugueiro, Folgosinho and the walled town of Linhares.

■ Head back to Coimbra via Seia on the edge of the park.

Route 2

The coastal route north of Lisbon covers great seaside resorts and the historical towns of the Estremadura region.

■ From Lisbon, head north to Ericeira (see p19). Continue up the coast road, past various swimming spots.

■ Stop off at Baleal, a tiny resort on an islet with a lovely beach. It is just beyond the large town of Peniche, where you can take a boat trip to the bird reserves on the Berlenga Islands.

■ Continue to Óbidos, a picture-book walled town with white-washed houses, given as a wedding present by the king of Portugal to his bride.

■ Swim at the fine beaches of São Martinho or Nazaré (see p19), before visiting Alcobaça, home to the twelfth-century monastery, once the most powerful in the country. Don't miss the kitchen, which once had a stream running through it to supply the monks with fresh fish.

■ Visit Fátima, one of the holiest towns in the Catholic world after children saw a vision of the Virgin Mary here. You can't miss its huge basilica and even more enormous esplanade, which holds over 100,000 during the main pilgrimages (see p29).

Route 3

This route follows the Tagus river from Lisbon through some beautiful towns and villages.

■ Drive from Lisbon to Santarém, an attractive town set on a cliff above the Tagus; don't miss the lovely churches of Marvila and Graça, or the view from the miradouro at the Portas do Sol.

■ Continue along the quieter south side of the Tagus, through bull-breeding country. Stop off at the sleepy town of Golegã, famous for its horse fair (see p29); don't miss its photographic museum in the wonderful house of Carlos Relvas.

■ Stop off in Constância, a dazzling white riverside village which was home to the famous poet, Camões. Go on to explore the lofty castle at Abrantes.

■ Finish up at Belver, a beautiful twelfth-century castle which once marked the northern edge of the Moorish kingdom.

Óbidos

Belver castle

Route 4

This route takes you deep into the traditional Alentejo district, with its white-washed villages and fortified frontier towns.

■ Take the road from Lisbon and cross the Tagus at Vila Franca, famous for its bull-running (see p29).

■ Cross the rolling cork groves of the Alentejo to Évora (see p20).

■ Continue to Estremoz, a rural town which comes alive with its Saturday market. Explore the old town walls or climb the tower of the Pousada de Santa Rainha Isabel for a great view of the surrounding lands.

■ Stop in Vila Viçosa, famous for its Paço Ducal, the holiday residence of the last kings of Portugal. Don't miss the vast kitchens, said to have been able to feed 700 people at a sitting.

kitchens at Paço Ducal

■ Drive on to Elvas, right on the Spanish border. Try and find your way through the perfectly preserved fortifications to the elegant Praça da República main square, and look out for the fifteenth-century towering Amoreira aqueduct which took over 100 years to complete.

■ Stop in Monsaraz, one of the prettiest of the fortified hilltop villages which line this section of the Portuguese border.

Elvas

The South

*T*he lower Alentejo is a flat, agricultural area containing some attractive white-washed towns and a craggy coastline which is slowly being discovered as an alternative seaside destination. Yet it is the Algarve, with a climate that remains fairly warm all year and a largely sheltered south-facing coastline, that remains the most popular holiday destination for Portuguese and foreign visitors alike. Portugal's southernmost district was the last part of Portugal to fall into Christian hands from the Moors, and to this day the Algarve's food and traditional buildings retain a Moorish influence. Sadly, many of the central coastal towns in particular have become unappealing high-rise developments. Nevertheless, if you do not mind summer crowds and prices somewhat above the rest of Portugal, the Algarve's climate and beaches are hard to beat. There are also old quarters of towns to be explored both along the coast and among the rolling hills of its interior, which are still more populated by orange and carob trees than people.

Don't miss

Towns and villages which make good bases

Lagos A fishing port and market town with good shops, bars and an attractive centre. It is near some fantastic sheltered coves and beaches which are ideal for children.
Salema This small white-washed fishing village, near a sandy beach, still has more colourful fishing boats than modern hotels.

Praia da Rocha

Albufeira One of the more developed Algarve towns, but ideal if you want a lively resort with great nightlife, good shopping, an old Moorish centre and a wonderful beach.

Vilamoura An up-market resort built around a marina, the place to go if you are into sports. It has a fine beach, offers yachting and golf and is near the tennis facilities and sports centres of Quinta do Lago and Vale do Lobo.

Tavira This attractive town, with riverside restaurants, is set slightly inland and remains as much a fishing town as a tourist destination. If you want a quieter base, Tavira has avoided over-development and offers easy access to the great beaches on the Ilha de Tavira.

Silves This is a good base if you want to escape the crowds of the coast yet remain in reach of the sea. Set in hills around six miles inland, Silves was the capital of the Moorish Algarve and remains the district's most interesting historical centre, with a castle, a cathedral and narrow cobbled streets leading down to cafés and bars along its riverfront.

Vila Nova de Milfontes The main resort on the Alentejo coast is bustling but low-rise, with some great seafood restaurants. The old town is next to a sheltered river estuary but within easy reach of some surf-beaten beaches.

Great beaches

Praia de Dona Ana, near Lagos, a dramatic sandy beach with safe swimming among its weird rock formations.

Albufeira The town beach gets crowded but remains impressive, lined with colourful fishing boats, while the nearby Praia da Falésia is quieter but equally spectacular.

Praia da Rocha This fantastic cliff-backed beach below a fort is understandably used by the Portuguese tourist board to promote the Algarve.

Armação da Pêra, a long stretch of beach which is a favourite for Portuguese holiday-makers.

Olhão This is the best place from which to reach the sand-spit islands, Ilha da Armona and Ilha da Culatra, the latter scattered with fishing communities. Both offer great swathes of pure sand.

Vilamoura, somewhat developed but the perfect spot for beach-lovers.

Ilha de Tavira, another sand-spit backed by dunes. Edged on one side by a mud-flats nature reserve, this is best reached from Tavira or the small complex at Pedras de El-Rei.

Porto Covo On the western Alentejo coast, this resort has sheltered cliff-backed coves to the north and a fine stretch of beach sheltered by an island to the south.

Praia de Santo André/Praia de Melides Two long sandy beaches up the Alentejo coast with natural lagoons, which offer safe swimming behind sand dunes when the sea gets too fearsome.

Praia de Marona

Daytrips and sights

■ Go to Caldas de Monchique, a lovely old spa town set amongst wooded hills which are ideal for walking and picnicking.

■ Visit Loulé, an attractive market town; explore the metalwork shops in its casbah-like centre and walk round the walls of its castle.

■ Walk or picnic in the Serra do Caldeirão, the rural mountainous area to the north of the region, largely deserted except for oak woods and sheep.

■ See the Roman remains at Milreu near Estói, where you can make out mosaics, the ruins of an ancient church and a bath house.

■ Visit Sagres and Cabo de São Vicente, the wild windswept western extremities of the Algarve,

considered the edge of the world in ancient times. Look out for Sagres' Rosa dos Ventos, a huge replica of the compass used by Henry the Navigator to open up the world to Portugal's great navigators of the fifteenth and sixteenth centuries.

■ Have lunch in Cacela Velha in the eastern Algarve. This tiny cliff-top village seems to be descended from a Greek island, and overlooks a great sand-spit; hitch a lift to it by boat for an afternoon swim.

■ Visit Vila Real, a lively border town designed in the same architectural style as the Baixa in Lisbon. Go up to Castro Marim, a sleepy town dwarfed by a castle which was the home to the knights of the Order of Christ.

■ Take a boat-trip up the Guadiana river, which separates Spain from Portugal, for a leisurely look at some unspoilt villages and countryside. Boat trips leave in summer from the harbour in Vila Real.

■ Head inland to the attractive border town of Alcoutim, on the Guadiana river, and onwards to Mértola, an attractive Alentejan hilltop town with a Moorish castle.

metalwork shop, Loulé

Madeira

This Atlantic island is nearer to Africa than Portugal, and experiences a moderate climate which makes it a good destination all year round. Its climate and volcanic soil have allowed plants brought in by traders from the east to thrive: bananas, mango, bird of paradise flowers and orchids are common, as are the vines which supply grapes for the famous Madeira fortified wines. The island has no big sandy beaches, but there are numerous pools for swimming in, while the mountainous interior is ideal for walking, along levadas, the old irrigation canals. Although Madeira is not a large island, car hire is recommended as bus services are not that useful.

Funchal, from Pico dos Barcelos

Don't miss

Funchal Stay in the island's capital and main town. Don't miss a stroll around the characterful Zona Velha old town. Visit the Quinta da Boavista orchid house in the Botanical Gardens.

Monte A hill town linked to Funchal by a steep cobbled street has the wicker toboggans, once used for farm goods, which now ferry passengers with the help of traditionally-dressed guides.

Câmara de Lobos One of the prettiest fishing villages on the island.

Cabo Girão A dizzy spot and the world's second highest sea cliff, amazingly cultivated in terraces.

Pico Ruivo Admire the views from the island's highest mountain at over 6500 feet.

Porto Moniz A safe and invigorating bathing spot, where the volcanic rock pools are naturally fed by the sea.

Porto Santo Take a daytrip to this neighbouring island with a superb sandy beach.

vegetable market, Funchal

Cabo Girão

Holidays, festivals and events

January New Year is welcomed in by a rowdy banging of pots and pans in every street, while the next day sees most restaurants chock-a-block. Funchal in Madeira welcomes the New Year with a spectacular fireworks display.

February Carnival procession in Lisbon, Loulé and other towns. Almond blossom in the inland Algarve and around Torre de Moncorvo in Trás-os-Montes. Film festival in Oporto.

March/April Easter. Celebrations are at their best in Braga (Minho) with its torch-lit processions.

April 25 Independence day, often welcomed in with fireworks, celebrating the relatively peaceful revolution of 1974.

April/May Flower festival in Madeira, a three-day event with floral displays and a parade.

May Queima das Fitas, Coimbra, lively celebrations marking the end of the university year.

May 1 Holiday.

May 13 Catholic pilgrimage to Fátima, Estremadura.

June Beer festival, Silves (Algarve). Portuguese soccer cup final (National Stadium, Lisbon, but if you can't get there, catch it on TV in any bar for a lively afternoon). Vaca Das Cordas, Ponte de Lima (Minho), a mini bull-running and street party. Agricultural fair, Santarém, with bull-fighting and street parties. Music festival in Funchal, Madeira.

June 10 Holiday.

June 13 Festas de Santo António. The best place to catch this saint's day is Lisbon, when the whole city becomes one big street party, especially around the Alfama.

June 24 Festas de São João. This saint's day is biggest in Oporto, where the centre of town becomes a mass of live bands, barbecues and people hitting each other with plastic hammers. Braga (Minho) also has extensive celebrations.

ıly Music festival, Estoril (near
ısbon). Bull-running, Vila Franca
 Xira (Ribatejo). Festival of Trays,
spectacular procession in Tomar
Ribatejo), but it only occurs every
ur years.

ugust Nossa Senhora da Agonia;
 e best place to catch the
 lebrations, processions and
 reworks is Viana do Castelo in the
 linho; or the fisherman's
 ocession in Póvoa do Varzim, near
 orto, with fireworks let off from
 shing boats.

ugust 15 Holiday.

eptember International music
 stival, various locations in the
 lgarve. Nossa Senhora dos
 emédios; the best place to catch the
 ocessions and pilgrimage is
 amego, Beira Alta. The New Fair,
 onte de Lima, with fireworks and
 irgrounds. Beginning of the port
 ne harvest along the river Douro.
 ine festival in Madeira, with wine
 sting and dancing.

October Bull-running, Vila Franca
de Xira (Ribatejo). Pilgrimage at
Fátima, Estremadura. Gastronomic
festival, Santarém (Ribatejo).

October 5 Holiday.

November 1 Holiday.

November 11 São Martinho, a
saint's day celebrated with chestnuts
and *água-pé*, a light wine. Catch the
horse fair in Golegã in Ribatejo,
which coincides with this date.

December Christmas Day tends
to be a family affair. Though less
commercialized than in some
countries, the lead-up to it can be
atmospheric and picturesque in
town centres. In the Beira Baixa,
you may see burning logs which
are traditionally kept alight outside
churches until Twelfth Night.

December 1 and 8 Holiday.

Bare necessities

Greetings

Hello!	**Olá!**
How are things?	**Como está?**
How do you do?	**Muito prazer**
Nice to meet you.	**Muito prazer em conhecê-lo.**
Fine, how are you?	**Bem, e você?**
Very well.	**Muito bem.**
Good morning.	**Bom dia.**
Good afternoon/evening.	**Boa tarde.**
Good evening/night.	**Boa noite.**
See you later.	**Até logo.**
See you tomorrow.	**Até amanhã.**
Bye.	**Adeus.**

Other useful words

Excuse me! (to attract attention)	**Desculpe!**
Please.	**Se faz favor.**
Thank you.	**Obrigado.** (said by men)/ **Obrigada**. (said by women)

Thank you very much.	**Muito obrigado/a.**
You're welcome.	**Não tem de quê.**
Excuse me. (to get by in a crowded place)	**Com licença.**
Sorry.	**Desculpe.**
It doesn't matter/It's all right.	**Tanto faz.**
yes/no	**sim/não**

(Is/Are) there . . . ?

Is there a lift?	**Há elevador?**
Are there any toilets?	**Há casas de banho?**

Where (is/are) . . . ?

Where is the town centre?	**Onde é o centro da cidade?**
Where are the fitting rooms?	**Onde são os provadores?**
É (à direita/à esquerda).	It's (on the right/on the left).
São (sempre em frente/no fim).	They're (straight on/at the end).

Do you have any . . . ?

Do you have any (unleaded petrol/prawns)?	**Tem (gasolina sem chumbo/ gambas)?**

How much . . . ?

How much does it cost?	**Quanto custa?**
How much are (the onions/the tomatoes) per kilo?	**Quanto custam (as cebolas/ os tomates) por quilo?**
How much is that?	**Quanto é isso?**
How much is that altogether?	**Quanto é tudo isso?**

I'd like . . .

I'd like (a shirt/a melon).	**Queria (uma camisa/um melão).**
I'd like a kilo of oranges.	**Queria um quilo de laranjas.**

Getting things straight

Pardon?	**Como disse?**
Could you say that again?	**Pode repetir isso?**
I don't understand.	**Não compreendo.**
More slowly, please.	**Mais devagar, se faz favor.**
What does it mean?	**O que quer dizer?**
Não sei.	I don't know.

About yourself

My name is . . .	**Chamo-me . . .**
I'm (Mr/Mrs/Miss) . . .	**Sou (o senhor/a senhora) . . .**
I'm from . . .	**Sou de . . .**
I'm a nurse.	**Sou enfermeiro** (male)/**enfermeir** (female).
I'm Irish.	**Sou irlandês** (male)/**irlandesa** (female).
I speak a little Portuguese.	**Falo um pouco de português.**
I'm here on (holiday/business).	**Estou aqui (de férias/ em negócios).**

Money

Local currency: **escudos**

5 escudos
25 escudos
50 escudos
100 escudos
500 escudos
1,000 escudos
2,000 escudos

Changing money

one pound (sterling)	**uma libra esterlina**
What's the exchange rate?	**Qual é o câmbio da libra?**
I want to change twenty (pounds/ dollars).	**Queria trocar vinte (libras/ dólares).**

Posso ver o seu passaporte?	May I see your passport?
A comissão que cobramos é . . .	The commission charge is . . .

The time

What time is it?	**Que horas são?**
What time do you (open/close)?	**A que horas (abre/fecha)?**
What time does it (leave/arrive)?	**A que horas (parte/chega)?**

It's one o'clock.	**É uma hora.**
It's two o'clock.	**São duas horas.**
It's ten past two.	**São duas e dez.**
It's quarter past two.	**São duas e um quarto.**
It's half past two.	**São duas e meia.**
It's twenty to three.	**São vinte para as três.**
It's a quarter to five.	**É um quarto para as cinco.**
13.20	**treze (horas) e vinte (minutos)**
at one o'clock	**à uma hora**
at two o'clock	**às duas horas**

Numbers

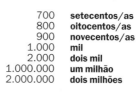

0	**zero**	11	**onze**
1	**um, uma**	12	**doze**
2	**dois, duas**	13	**treze**
3	**três**	14	**catorze**
4	**quatro**	15	**quinze**
5	**cinco**	16	**dezasseis**
6	**seis**	17	**dezassete**
7	**sete**	18	**dezoito**
8	**oito**	19	**dezanove**
9	**nove**	20	**vinte**
10	**dez**	21	**vinte e um/a**

22	**vinte e dois, duas**	700	**setecentos/as**
30	**trinta**	800	**oitocentos/as**
40	**quarenta**	900	**novecentos/as**
50	**cinquenta**	1.000	**mil**
60	**sessenta**	2.000	**dois mil**
70	**setenta**	1.000.000	**um milhão**
80	**oitenta**	2.000.000	**dois milhões**
90	**noventa**		
100	**cem, cento**		
101	**cento e um/a**		
110	**cento e dez**		
200	**duzentos/as**		
201	**duzentos/as e um/a**		
300	**trezentos/as**		
400	**quatrocentos/as**		
500	**quinhentos/as**		
600	**seiscentos/as**		

Countries and nationalities

America	a **América, americano/a**
Australia	a **Austrália, australiano/a**
Austria	a **Áustria, austríaco/a**
Belgium	a **Bélgica, belga**
Brazil	o **Brasil, brasileiro/a**
Canada	o **Canadá, canadense**
China	a **China, chinês/esa**
Denmark	a **Dinamarca, dinamarquês/esa**
England	a **Inglaterra, inglês/esa**
Finland	a **Finlândia, finlandês/esa**
France	a **França, francês/esa**
Germany	a **Alemanha, alemão, alemã**
Great Britain	a **Grã-Bretanha, britânico/a**
Greece	a **Grécia, grego/a**
Holland	a **Holanda, holandês/esa**

Hong Kong	o **Hong Kong, chinês/esa de Hong Kong**
India	a **Índia, indiano/a**
Ireland	a **Irlanda, irlandês/esa**
Italy	a **Itália, italiano/a**
Japan	o **Japão, japonês/esa**
Luxembourg	o **Luxemburgo, luxemburguês/esa**
Netherlands	a **Holanda, holandês/esa**
New Zealand	a **Nova Zelândia, neozelandês/esa**
Northern Ireland	a **Irlanda do Norte, da Irlanda do Norte**
Norway	a **Noruega, norueguês/esa**
Portugal	o **Portugal, português/esa**
Russia	a **Rússia, russo/a**
Scotland	a **Escócia, escocês/esa**
South Africa	a **África do Sul, sul-africano/a**
Spain	a **Espanha, espanhol/a**
Sweden	a **Suécia, sueco/a**
Switzerland	a **Suíça, suíço/a**
United States	os **Estados Unidos, americano/a**
Wales	o **País de Gales, galês/esa**

CAMBIO

CHANGE
EXCHANGE
WECHSEL

ÁFRICA DO SUL
ALEMANHA
AUSTRÁLIA
ÁUSTRIA
BÉLGICA
CANADÁ
UNIÃO EUROPEIA
DINAMARCA
ESPANHA
E.U.A.
FINLÂNDIA
FRANÇA
GRÉCIA
HOLANDA
INGLATERRA
IRLANDA
ITÁLIA
JAPÃO
LUXEMBURGO
NORUEGA
SUÉCIA
SUIÇA
VENEZUELA

Days

Monday	**segunda-feira**		Sunday	**domingo**
Tuesday	**terça-feira**		today	**hoje**
Wednesday	**quarta-feira**		yesterday	**ontem**
Thursday	**quinta-feira**		tomorrow	**amanhã**
Friday	**sexta-feira**			
Saturday	**sábado**			

Months

January	**Janeiro**
February	**Fevereiro**
March	**Março**
April	**Abril**
May	**Maio**
June	**Junho**
July	**Julho**
August	**Agosto**
September	**Setembro**

October	**Outubro**
November	**Novembro**
December	**Dezembro**

Colours

black	**preto/a**		purple	**púrpura**
blue	**azul**		red	**vermelho/a**
brown	**castanho/a**		white	**branco/a**
green	**verde**		yellow	**amarelo/a**
grey	**cinzento/a**		light	**claro/a**
orange	**cor-de-laranja**		dark	**escuro/a**
pink	**cor-de-rosa**			

Alphabet

In Portuguese, the letters of the alphabet are pronounced as follows.

A	(ah)	M	(emm)
B	(beh)	N	(enn)
C	(seh)	O	(o)
D	(deh)		as in 'boat'
E	(eh)	P	(peh)
F	(effe)	Q	(keh)
G	(zheh)	R	(air)
	'zh' like 's'	S	(ess)
	in 'pleasure'	T	(teh)
H	(er-*gar*)	U	(oo)
I	(ee)	V	(veh)
J	(zhota)	W	(veh *doo*-ploo)
	'zh' like 's'	X	(sheesh)
	in 'pleasure'	Y	(*eep*-see-lon)
K	(kappa)	Z	(zeh)
L	(ell)		

Language works

Greetings

1 Greeting a neighbour on the
way to the shops
■ Olá!
□ Olá! Como está?
■ Bem, e você?
□ Muito bem, obrigado. Até
  amanhã!
■ Adeus!

When do you expect to see your
neighbour again?

How much . . . ?

2 Buying onions at the market
■ Boa tarde.
□ Boa tarde. Há cebolas?
■ Há, sim.
□ Queria dois quilos.
■ Dois quilos.
□ Quanto é?
■ Cem escudos.
□ Obrigado, adeus.
■ Adeus, boa tarde.

Is it morning or afternoon? How much
are onions a kilo?

Money

3 Changing money
■ Bom dia.
□ Bom dia. Qual é o câmbio da
  libra?
■ A duzentos e quarenta escudos.
□ Queria trocar vinte libras.
■ Muito bem. O passaporte, se faz
  favor.

How much would you get, approx-
imately, for your twenty pounds?

Try it out

The numbers game

dois + quatro =
sete − dois =
um x três =
dez ÷ cinco =
seis + onze + treze =
oitocentos − quinhentos =
duzentos x cinquenta =
dois milhões ÷ mil =

Where are we now?

Write down the Portuguese word
for each country:
a The two most westerly
  countries in Europe.
b It sent an Armada to invade
  England in 1588.
c It could be described as a
  boot-shaped peninsula.
d It used to be divided into East
  and West.
e It used to be known as British
  North America.
f The world's largest exporter o
  coffee.
g The two countries connected
  by the Channel Tunnel.
h The English-speaking country
  with a large Spanish-speaking
  population.

Times

What's the time in Portuguese?
a 7.30
b 10.15
c 20.20
d 15.10

As if you were there

You're looking for the bank
o banco).
(Say excuse me, good morning)
Bom dia.
(Ask where the bank is)
Sempre em frente . . . à direita.
(Ask what time it closes)
Às duas horas.
(Thank her)
Não tem de quê. Adeus.
(Say goodbye)

Sound Check

at the beginning of a word or
after a consonant, like 's' in
'sun':
Se faz favor (**se** sounds like 'sir')
(Please)

between vowels, like 'z' in
'oo':
Há casas de banho? (**casas**
sounds like '**car**-zersh')
(Are there any toilets?)

s at the end of a word or before
'c', 'f', 'p', 'q' or 't', like 'sh' in
'shed':
Como está? (**está** sounds like
'eesh-**tah**')
(How are you?)

**Talking through your nose (nasal
sounds)**
You make this sound when:
a vowel has a 'til' (~) over it
não (sounds like 'now')
(no)
a vowel is followed by 'm' or
'n', especially at the end of a
word:
sim (sounds like 'see')
(yes)

Practise the sound in these
words:
**são , não, bem, bom, custam, um,
cem**

a sounds like 'er' or 'a' in
'asleep', and **o** sounds like 'oo',
when they're at the ends of
words, or if they're not in the
stressed position:
obrigada ('thank you', said by a
woman) sounds like 'oo-bri-**gar**-
der'
obrigado ('thank you', said by a
man) sounds like 'oo-bri-**gar**-
doo'

Getting around

Road crossings

The best of the connecting roads from Spain are those which link the border at Valença to Oporto; Vilar Formoso to Aveiro; and Huelva/Vila Real to the Algarve. There are also frequent coach services to Oporto and Lisbon from Paris, Madrid and other cities in Spain which are near the Portuguese border.

Airports

Portugal's international airports are in Oporto for the north, Lisbon for the centre, and Faro for the Algarve and the south. You may find flights cheapest to Faro, where it is relatively easy to catch onward bus services to most Portuguese towns. Madeira's airport is near Santa Cruz, a short ride from Funchal. All the airports have regular bus connections to the town centres; a taxi is also a relatively cheap option.

Railways

Most train services from Europe go via Madrid to Lisbon. The route via the central border town of Vilar Formoso, for Coimbra and Oporto, is another option. There are also local connections from Galicia in Spain to Valença and Oporto in the north; from Badajoz and Elvas for southern central Portugal; and from Huelva and Vila Real for the Algarve. None of these routes, however, is particularly fast.

Car or motorbike hire

Hiring a car or motorbike is a relatively inexpensive option. Car hire companies are represented in all of Portugal's main airports and in most major towns and resorts.

Portugal has invested heavily in a road-building programme in recent years, and it is worth paying to travel on the growing number of fast A toll motorways, especially between Lisbon and Oporto and across the Algarve.

Remember that Portugal has a notoriously high accident rate, mainly because the poor state of many roads does not deter fast driving and reckless overtaking. Take great care at all times. In towns, you may find parking centrally is problematic, while congestion in Oporto and Lisbon is particularly bad.

I'd like to hire a car.
Queria alugar um carro.

Road travel at a glance
A roads Toll roads, generally fast and uncrowded dual carriageways with regular service stations. Speed limit: usually 75mph.
IP roads Fast roads, much the same as A roads but without the tolls so tend to be much more crowded.
IC/EN Major main roads, usually with one lane each way and sections of dual carriageway. Often busy; watch out for slow lorries. Speed limit: 56mph.
N roads Main roads, usually one lane each way, often busy but the best way to see Portuguese towns and villages. Look out for slow local traffic including bicycles, mopeds and horses and carts. Speed limit: 56mph/31mph in urban areas.

Petrol Prices for *super* (standard petrol) and *sem chumbo* (unleaded) are slightly more expensive than most European countries. Most petrol stations open from 8 am to midnight.
Breakdowns The *Automóvel Clube de Portugal* has a reciprocal agreement with members of some automobile clubs in Europe (see p100). Generally, costs for repairs are inexpensive.

Buses

Portugal is not a big country, and if you plan to stick to visiting major towns and resorts, you will find the various privately run bus services reasonably priced, reliable and fairly fast. Larger towns have a central bus station where you can get tickets and details of times; otherwise, check in the local tourist office or a central café. You can usually pay once you have boarded the bus if necessary. For more out-of-the-way places, such as between smaller villages in Beira Alta and Beira Baixa and Trás-os-Montes, many local bus routes have been rationalized and you may find yourself relying on very infrequent services.

What time is the bus to . . .?
A que horas é o autocarro para . . .?

Trains

Portugal's rail network has been largely neglected in recent times, and though extremely cheap, rail travel can be tortuously slow, with stations often several kilometres from the town name they represent. If you really want to get around quickly, the only worthwhile train is the Alfa which connects Lisbon with Oporto via Coimbra. If you enjoy the atmosphere of leisurely rail travel, some routes are hard to beat, especially in the north of Portugal.

Unmissable rail routes

■ The breezy coastal route from Oporto to Valença (2–3½ hours) via Viana do Castelo.
■ The scenic inland river valley route from Oporto to Amarante (2 hours).
■ Oporto to Régua, through port wine-growing country along the Douro (2–2½ hours).
■ Régua to Vila Real in Trás-os-Montes (1 hour), a tiny single-track train following a steep river valley, passing through vineyards and people's back gardens!

Régua to Vila Real

Train travel at a glance
Regional The slowest local trains which stop at all stations. Usually extremely cheap.
Inter-regional These are slightly faster than *Regionais* although they cost the same, stopping at intermediate stations only.
Intercidade You will pay slightly more for these inter-city trains, which are your best option if time is important.
Alfa The most expensive but fastest service from Lisbon to Coimbra (2–2½ hours) and Oporto (3–4 hours). Make sure you reserve tickets in advance, as this comfortable service gets quickly booked up.

Alfa train

Tickets
Buy a ticket before you catch a train, unless you board from an unmanned station in which case the ticket inspector should not fine you!

Discounts and passes
■ Children under twelve pay 50% of the full fare.
■ Toddlers under four travel for free.
■ Senior citizens over 60 pay 60% of the full fare.
■ A *cartão de família* rail pass is good value if you plan to travel widely by rail with your family.
■ A *bilhete turístico* tourist rail pass is worthwhile if you plan to travel extensively by train; valid for one, two or three weeks.

Can you tell me where to get off?
Pode avisar-me onde devo descer?

Other options

■ Taxis are relatively inexpensive in Portugal, and you may be able to negotiate a reasonable rate for a day or half-day's tour of local sites.
■ Cycling is growing in popularity as a pastime, especially around the flat coastal areas, but remember to keep a look-out for cars! Ask in the local tourist office for local bike hire companies.

Ferries and boats

Within Portugal, there are ferries which link Lisbon with the south of the river Tagus at Cacilhas or Montijo, bypassing the suspension bridge, and Setúbal over the river Sado with the Tróia peninsula. These ferries offer an alternative scenic, if less rapid, route south.

Leisure trips
■ There is a regular summer ferry from Peniche to the Atlantic Berlenga islands, a popular destination for campers and bird watchers.
■ Organized boat trips travel up the Guadiana from Vila Real in the Algarve.
■ You can take yacht and boat cruises on the Atlantic from Algarve resorts such as Vilamoura and Lagos.
■ Boat trips and cruises go up the river Douro from Oporto or Régua, and up the Tagus from Lisbon.

City transport

It is best to buy a block of tickets for buses from kiosks, which works out far cheaper than if you buy a ticket on the bus itself. Each ticket has two *módulos*, allowing two one-zone journeys or one trip across two zones. Most major towns have a good network of buses. Bus routes are usually shown on the orange bus stops. Press the button when you wish to get off at the next stop.

Trams and funiculars

Tickets

With all forms of public transport, make sure you punch (*oblitere*) your ticket before your journey. Machines are just before the platforms in commuter train stations and on the metro, or just inside the door of trams and buses.

Passes

You can buy a tourist pass for four or seven days from city kiosks, valid on buses, trams and, in Lisbon, on metro trains.

Buses

The British-made pre-war *eléctrico* trams are amongst Oporto's and Lisbon's most distinctive features, the perfect way to negotiate steep and narrow hills. Unfortunately their sluggish pace and tendency to get halted by poorly parked cars has meant many routes have been curtailed, and Oporto now has only one central route. To identify tram stops, follow the overhead power lines and look for the *Carris* company sign. *Carris* also run Lisbon's *elevadores* (funiculars), which are short railways and lifts. Buy blocks of tickets valid on the trams and the funiculars in Lisbon from kiosks.

Sé Catedral
Jardim do Paço

Phrasemaker
Asking the way

Excuse me! (to attract attention)	**Desculpe!**
Which way is (the beach/ the Tourist Office)?	**Para (a praia/o Posto de Turismo)?**
Is there a bank near here?	**Há um banco perto daqui?**
Are there any large shops near here?	**Há lojas grandes perto daqui?**
Where is the castle?	**Onde fica o castelo?**
Is it far?	**Fica longe?**

Aí (é).	There (it is).
Sempre em frente.	Carry straight on.
Vire à (direita/esquerda).	Turn (right/left).
Atravesse a (ponte/estrada principal).	Cross the (bridge/main road).
À (direita/esquerda).	On the (left/right).
A (primeira/segunda) rua . . .	The (first/second) street . . .
Até a . . .	As far as . . .
A cem metros	100 metres away
Fica a uns trinta quilómetros.	It's about 30 km away.
É (bastante) (perto/longe).	It's (fairly) (close/far away).
(perto/em frente/atrás)	(near/opposite/behind)
no fim da rua	at the end of the street
na esquina	on the corner

Places to look for

airport	o aeroporto	bus stop	a paragem do autocarro
bank	o banco	castle	o castelo
beach	a praia	cathedral	a catedral
bridge	a ponte	chemist's	a farmácia
bus station	a estação de autocarros	church	a igreja
		hospital	o hospital
		market	o mercado, a praça
		mosque	a mesquita
		museum	o museu
		park	o parque
		police station	a esquadra de polícia
		port	o porto
		railway station	a estação de caminho de ferro
		shop	a loja

Portugal

50
90
100
120

shopping area	**a zona comercial**		temple	**o templo**
square	**o largo, a praça**		toilet	**a casa de banho**
stadium	**o estádio**		town centre	**o centro da cidade**
street	**a rua**			
swimming pool	**a piscina**		underground station	**a estação de metro**

Vehicles

			funicular	**o elevador**
			hydrofoil	**o hidroplano**
bike	**a bicicleta**		motorbike	**a motocicleta**
boat	**o barco**		plane	**o avião**
bus	**o autocarro**		taxi	**o táxi**
car	**o carro**		train	**o comboio**
coach	**a camioneta**		tram	**o eléctrico**
ferry	**o ferry-boat**		underground	**o metro**
flight	**o vôo**			

Hiring a car or bike

I'd like to hire a car.	**Queria alugar um carro**
a (small/medium/large) car	**um carro (pequeno/médio/grande)**
How much does it cost per (day/week)?	**Quanto é por (dia/semana)?**
(See p33 for numbers.)	
Is insurance included?	**Está incluído o seguro?**
Por quanto tempo?	For how long?
A sua carta de condução, se faz favor.	Your driving licence, please.
O sinal é . . .	The deposit is . . .

Getting petrol

30 litres of unleaded	**trinta litros de sem chumbo**
1,000 escudos' worth of 4-star	**mil escudos de super**
Fill up with diesel, please.	**Encha com gasóleo, se faz favor.**
Can you check the (air/water/oil)?	**Pode verificar (o ar/a água/o óleo)?**

43

Roadside information

Where are we on the map?	**Onde ficamos no mapa?**
How far is . . .?	**A quantos quilómetros fica . . .?**
(See p33 for numbers.)	
Is this the road to . . .?	**É este o caminho para . . .?**

Road signs

acenda os faróis	use headlights
autoestrada	motorway
centro cidade	city centre
dê prioridade	give priority
desvio	diversion
devagar	slowly
estacionamento permitido	parking allowed
este	east
mantenha-se pela direita	keep right
não ultrapassar	no overtaking
norte	north
obras	road works
oeste	west
olhe . . .	look . . .
peagem	toll
peões	pedestrians
perigo	danger
portagem	toll
proibido estacionar	parking forbidden
sem saída	no through road
sentido proibido	no access
sul	south
zona para peões	pedestrian zone

Using the underground

Two tickets, please.	**Dois bilhetes, se faz favor.**
A booklet of ten, please.	**Uma caderneta de dez, se faz favor.**
Does this train go to . . .?	**Este metro vai para . . .?**

Tome (a linha/o número) . . .	Take (line/number) . . .
Tem de (mudar/descer) na próxima paragem.	You need to (change/get off) at the next stop.

Getting information on trains and buses

Are there (buses/trains) to . . . ?	**Há (autocarros/comboios) para . . . ?**
What time is the bus to . . . ?	**A que horas é o autocarro para . . . ?**
What time is the next one?	**A que horas é o próximo?**
Does this train go to . . . ?	**Este comboio vai para . . . ?**
Is it direct?	**É directo?**
Where is the connection?	**Onde é a ligação?**
From which platform?	**De que cais/linha?**
At what time does it arrive?	**A que horas chega?**
How long does it take?	**Quanto tempo demora?**
When does the last one come back?	**A que horas regressa o último?**
Have you got a timetable?	**Tem horário?**
Can you tell me where to get off?	**Pode avisar-me onde devo descer?**

Desça em . . .	Get off at . . .
Mude em . . .	Change at . . .

Buying a ticket

Where is the ticket office?	**Onde é a bilheteira?**
A return ticket, please.	**Um bilhete de ida e volta, se faz favor.**
A single ticket, please.	**Um bilhete simples, se faz favor.**
for two adults and one child	**para dois adultos e uma criança**
first/second class	**primeira/segunda classe**
to . . .	**para . . .**
a (family rail pass/tourist rail pass)	**um (cartão de família/bilhete turístico)**
I'd like to reserve (a seat/a couchette).	**Queria reservar (um lugar/uma couchette).**

Fumadores ou não fumadores?	Smoking or non-smoking?
Há um suplemento de . . .	There is a supplement of . . .
Oblitere o seu bilhete.	Punch your ticket (see p41).

• WC/Duche 🚻
Ag. Com. de Passageiros-Porto
Multibanco **MB**
Consignas Automaticas 🔒🔒
Bar e Restaurante 🍸 🍴
Auto Expresso 🚌 200m
Parque Alfa **P** 200m

Signs

alfândega	customs
cais	platform
câmbio	exchange
Caminhos de Ferro Portugueses (CP)	Portuguese Railways
check-in	check-in
chegadas	arrivals
controlo de passaportes	passport control
controlo de segurança	security check
depósito de baggagens	left-luggage
destino	destination
dias úteis	weekdays
entrada	entrance
linha	platform
partidas	departures
perdidos e achados	lost property
porta/portão	gate
saída	exit
sala de espera	waiting room

reduza a velocidade:
•ESCOLA

Taking a taxi

Is there a taxi rank round here?	**Há uma praça de táxis perto daqui?**
To (the airport), please.	**Para (o aeroporto), se faz favor.**
To this address . . .	**Para este endereço . . .**
How long will it take?	**Quanto tempo demora?**
How far is it?	**A que distância é?**
Stop here.	**Pare aqui.**
How much (is that/will it be)?	**Quanto (é/será)?**
I'd like a receipt.	**Queria um recibo.**
Keep the change.	**Guarde o troco.**
This is for you.	**Isto é para o senhor/a senhora.** *
(*See p111 for how to say 'you'.)	

Não demora muito.	Not long.
Não é longe.	Not far.

Language works

Asking the way

A passer-by helps you get to the cathedral.
Para a catedral?
É na segunda rua à esquerda.
Fica no fim.

You have to take the . . . street on the . . . It's at the . . .

Getting petrol

On the right road?
Vinte litros de super, se faz favor.
Muito bem. Mais alguma coisa?
É este o caminho para Évora?
É, sim. Fica a uns trinta quiló-metros.

You are going the wrong way: true/ false?

Monforte 24
Portalegre 53

Getting information on trains and buses

A day in the country
Há autocarros para Loulé?
Há, sim. Há um cada hora.
A que horas regressa o último?
Às sete horas.
cada hora = every hour)

You can stay there until . . . o'clock.

Catching a taxi

Your train leaves twenty minutes.
Para a estação,
se faz favor. É longe?
Não é longe. Fica a dez minutos.

Will you make it on time? Yes or no?

Try it out

Wordsearch

There are ten types of transport hidden here. Words go up and down, backwards, forwards and diagonally.

A	D	X	U	S	F	O	X	H	B
H	V	E	C	A	R	R	O	I	U
M	O	I	O	B	M	O	C	D	Y
E	S	F	A	S	G	I	N	R	T
T	A	R	G	O	C	D	X	O	F
R	C	N	I	L	M	W	B	P	N
O	I	X	E	U	B	Q	U	L	E
R	A	T	E	N	O	I	M	A	C
T	A	U	B	R	U	S	D	N	Y
A	U	T	O	C	A	R	R	O	M

Locations

All these words for places to visit have been broken up. Can you match the beginnings with the ends?

BAN	ÇA	MUS	ÇÃO
CAST	IA	ESTA	GO
PRA	CO	PRA	ELO
		LAR	EU

AR - ÁGUA

Sound Check

g followed by 'e' or 'i' and **j** sound like 's' in 'pleasure':
　　longe (far) sounds
　　like '**lorn**-zhee'
　　loja (shop) sounds
　　like '**loh**-zher'.

ç sounds like 's' in 'sun':
　　estação (station) sounds like
　　'eesh-ta-**sow**' – and the 'sow' is
　　said through the nose, because
　　of the 'til' (~) on the 'a'.
　　praça (square) sounds like
　　'**prar**-sser'

Somewhere to stay

At a glance

■ Book beforehand in major resorts and in the summer months.
■ Contact your local Portuguese tourist board for a list of recommended hotels, *pousadas* (see below), villas and manor houses.
■ If you do not have a reservation, ask for advice at a local tourist office, or ask to see any room before you take it.
■ If you cannot find pillows or extra blankets in your room, look in the wardrobe or cupboard.
■ Bathroom and toilet light switches are usually on the outside.
■ Remember not to put any paper – not even toilet paper – in the toilets of older buildings: use the bin provided.

Types of accommodation

Portugal has a wide range of accommodation, although it is a good idea to book up beforehand to be guaranteed the accommodation you want in the summer months. Most of the Algarve and other coastal resorts can offer either self-catering, hotel, camping or private room accommodation; in more out-of-the-way places, your options may be limited to a guest house or private rooms. Tourist offices can provide a list of local accommodation and may be able to phone for you to check availability and prices.

Do you have a double room for two nights?
Tem um quarto duplo para duas noites?

Children

Most types of accommodation cater for children of all ages, but it is advisable to check beforehand if possible, especially if you intend to stay in smaller guest houses. Children under eight are entitled to 50% discount in hotels if they share a room with you. Cots can generally be arranged if the hotel is notified in advance.

Self-catering

With excellent fresh food available from most shops and markets, self-catering can make a pleasant option especially if you have your own garden, patio and barbecue facilities. The Portuguese tourist board, local tourist offices and many travel agencies can supply lists of self-catering apartments and villas throughout Portugal. Self-catering particularly prevalent in the Algarve although apartments and villas tend to be more suitable for groups of at least four people. If you want a particular type of place, such as one with a pool or near the coast, make sure you book up well in advance. Check transport connections if you do not have a car as you could be some way from the shops.

Hotels

Most people find eating out as cheap as self-catering, especially outside the Algarve, so if you want to avoid the hassle of cooking, staying in a hotel can be a comfortable option. Hotels in Portugal are graded from one to five stars. One- to three-star hotels are usually good value, often with a TV and usually with en-suite facilities. Prices should include breakfast. Four- and five-star hotels, along with the sometimes character-ful *estalagens* and *albergarias* (inns), offer all the facilities expected of a good international hotel, with prices to match.

How much is it per night?
Quanto é por noite?

Pousadas

Pousadas are up-market hotels, usually in converted historic buildings. These can be expensive, but if you are tempted by the option of staying in a historic town house (such as in Guimarães), a former castle (such as in Óbidos), or monastery (such as in Évora), *pousadas* are for you. Some of them

are in out-of-the-way places (such sas São Bento in Gerês), so you may need your own transport, but they invariably come with good-quality restaurants. For a list of the 39 *pousadas*, contact ENATUR in Lisbon (01 848 1221) or your local Portuguese tourist board.

Country houses and manor houses

Privately-let country and manor houses offer visitors another chance to stay in some characterful Portuguese buildings. These can vary from simple farm buildings to lavish mansions with swimming pools, some in town centres and others in remote rural areas. Breakfast is included, and you can often choose to have an evening meal with the host family, some of whom will be the perfect source of local information. Details can be supplied by your local Portuguese tourist board, or by one of the organizations which market such accommodation throughout Portugal: TURIHAB (Ponte de Lima 058 741672), PRIVETUR (Ponte de Lima 058 741493) or ANTER (Évora 066 744555).

Guest houses and private rooms

A *pensão* is a privately-run guest house which is graded by the tourist board. Room prices should be displayed on the back of each bedroom door. Facilities vary widely; the better ones come complete with en-suite bathrooms, TV and (in winter) central heating and are as good as many hotels, with substantial breakfasts included. Other *pensões* are much more basic, with a separate bath or shower or even just a jug of water and a basin in your sparse room. Nevertheless, most come at a very reasonable rate by European standards. Other variants on the *pensão* are the *residencial* or the slightly more basic *hospedaria* or *casa de hóspede* hostel.

Another option is to stay in a room in a private house. Look for windows displaying a *quartos* or *dormidas* sign and ring on the bell. The local tourist office can also direct you to these, or you may find owners approaching you in the street to offer you a room. Make sure you see the room before you take it, and agree on a price beforehand. Prices should work out cheaper than *pensões*.

What time is breakfast?
A que horas é o pequeno almoço?

Camping and youth hostels

If you hold an International Youth Hostel card, you can stay in one of Portugal's 19 youth hostels, some of which are in great locations, although price-wise they are little cheaper than staying in a *pensão*.

If you want to stay in some of Portugal's beauty spots, there are several campsites, most of which are very reasonably priced. Not all are very large, however, so shared facilities can get busy in the summer months. Some sites will also request an international camping carnet (available from camping organizations in most countries). A list of campsites can be supplied by your local Portuguese tourist board, or contact the Orbitur chain of campsites (Lisbon 01 815 4871).

Camping wild is possible (though often disapproved of) in rural Portugal, but it is advisable to check first with a local tourist office as there have been isolated attacks on campers. Camping wild in the Algarve is not recommended as thefts are not uncommon.

Phrasemaker
Finding a place

Is there a (hotel/campsite/youth hostel) near here?	**Há um (hotel/parque de campismo/pousada da juventude) aqui perto?**
Do you have a (single/double/family) room?	**Tem um quarto (individual/duplo/para uma família)?**
for two nights	**para duas noites**
(See p33 for numbers.)	
For four people – two adults and two children.	**Para quatro pessoas – dois adultos e duas crianças.**
May I see the room?	**Posso ver o quarto?**
How much is it per night?	**Quanto é por noite?**
Don't you have anything cheaper?	**Não tem nada mais barato?**
I'll take it.	**Fico com ele.**
I'll let you know/We'll see.	**Ainda não sei/Aviso depois.**
Quantas noites?	How many nights?
Quantas pessoas?	How many people?
Lamento, o hotel está cheio.	I'm sorry, the hotel is full.

Specifications

with (bathroom/shower/cot)	**com (casa de banho/duche/cama de bebé)**
with (a single/a double) bed	**com uma cama (individual/de casal)**
half board	**meia pensão**
Is breakfast included?	**Está incluído o pequeno almoço?**
Is value-added tax included?	**Está incluído o IVA?** (say 'ee-ver')
O (pequeno almoço/IVA) (está incluído/não está incluído).	(Breakfast/tax) is (included/not included).

Types of accommodation

beds	**as camas**
campsite	**o parque de campismo**
flat	**o apartamento**
flats/apartments to let	**os apartamentos para alugar**
guest house	**a pensão**
hotel	**o hotel**
rooms to let	**os quartos/as dormidas**
youth hostel	**a pousada de juventude**

a albergaria	inn
a casa de hóspede	hostel
as dormidas	rooms to let
a estalagem	inn
a hospedaria	hostel
a pousada	up-market hotel (see p49)
os quartos	rooms to let
o residencial	hotel

Checking in

I have a reservation.	**Mandei reservar.**
My name is . . .	**Chamo-me . . .**
Where can I park?	**Onde posso estacionar?**

Qual é o seu nome, se faz favor?	Your name, please?
Posso ver o seu passaporte?	May I see your passport?
Queira preencher esta ficha, se faz favor.	Please fill in the form.
O quarto número . . .	Room number . . .
Qual é a matrícula do seu carro?	What is your car registration number? (See p33 for numbers.)

Services

What time is breakfast?	**A que horas é o pequeno almoço?**
Is there (a lift/air conditioning)?	**Há (elevador/ar condicionado)?**
Do you have an iron?	**Tem ferro?**
Where is the (restaurant/ bar)?	**Onde é o (restaurante/bar)?**
How do I get an outside number?	**Como marco uma ligação exterior?**

Das sete e meia às dez e meia.	From 7.30 to 10.30. (See p33 for clock times.)
É ao lado da piscina.	It's next to the swimming pool.
Marque zero.	Dial zero.

Facilities

air conditioning	o ar condicionado	patio	o pátio
balcony	a varanda	restaurant	o restaurante
bar	o bar	room service	o serviço de quartos
bathroom	a casa de banho	safe	o cofre
breakfast	o pequeno almoço	safe deposit box	o cofre/a caixa forte
car park	o parque de estacionamento	sauna	a sauna
double room	o quarto duplo	single room	o quarto simples/individual
family room	o quarto para uma familia	shower	o duche
fitness centre	o ginásio	swimming pool	a piscina
garden	o jardim	telephone	o telefone
laundry service	o serviço de lavandaria	tennis court	o campo de ténis
lift	o ascensor/elevador	terrace	o terraço
minibar	o minibar	trouser press	a passadeira de calças
		view	a vista

ELEVADORES	⇧
FITNESS CENTER / SAUNAS	⇧
SALAS DE REUNIÕES	⇧
PISCINAS	⇧
TÉNIS	⇧
SURF BAR	⇦
RESTAURANTE OCEANO	⇦
TABACARIA / GIFT SHOP	⇧

Problems

(The telephone/The shower) isn't working.	**(O telefone/O duche) não funciona.**
There is a problem with (the telephone/ the shower).	**Há um problema com (o telefone/ o duche).**
How do you work (the shower/ the blind)?	**Como funciona (o duche/ o estore)?**
There is no (soap/water).	**Não há (sabonete/água).**
There are no (towels/pillows/ blankets).	**Não há (toalhas/almofadas/ cobertores).**

Mando alguém.	I'll send somebody.
Vou buscá-los.	I'll get you them.

In your room

adaptor	**o adaptador**	key	**a chave**
air conditioning	**o ar condicio-nado**	lamp	**a lâmpada**
		luggage	**a bagagem**
blankets	**os cobertores**	pillow	**a almofada**
blinds (inside window)	**os estores**	pillow case	**a fronha**
cold water	**a água fria**	plug (socket)	**a tomada**
curtain	**a cortina**	radio	**o rádio**
door	**a porta**	television	**a televisão**
hairdryer	**o secador de cabelo**	toilet paper	**o papel higiénico**
handle	**o puxador**	towel	**a toalha**
hot water	**a água quente**	washbasin	**o lavatório**

Asking for help

Have you got a safety deposit box?	**Tem cofre?**
Do you have a plan of the town?	**Tem uma planta da vila?**
Could you order me a taxi?	**Pode-me chamar um táxi?**
I'd like an alarm call at . . .	**Queria uma chamada para acordar-me às . . .**

(See p33 for clock times.)

Checking out

I'd like to pay the bill.	**Queria pagar a conta.**
by (traveller's cheque/ credit card)	**com (traveller's cheques/cartão de crédito)**
in cash	**em dinheiro**
I think there is a mistake.	**Creio que se enganou na conta.**

Qual é o número do seu quarto?	What is your room number?
Como vai pagar?	How are you going to pay?
Assine aqui.	Sign here.

Campsites

Have you got space for a (car/ caravan/tent)?	**Tem lugar para (um carro/ uma caravana/uma tenda)?**
How much does it cost?	**Qual é o preço?**
Where are the (showers/ toilets/dustbins)?	**Onde são (os duches/as casas de banho/os caixotes do lixo)?**
Is there a (laundry/shop/ swimming pool)?	**Há (lavandaria/loja/piscina)?**

Temos um lugar livre para três noites.	We have a pitch free for three nights.

Self-catering

I've rented a villa.	**Aluguei uma casa.**
How does the (heating/ water) work?	**Como funciona (o aquecimento/ a água)?**

Language works

Finding a place

1 You are travelling without a reservation.
- **Tem um quarto duplo?**
- □ **Quantas noites?**
- **Para três noites.**

What does the receptionist want to find out?

2 Decision time!
- **Quanto é por noite?**
- □ **Oito mil escudos.**
- **Não tem nada mais barato?**
- □ **Não, senhor.**
- **Fico com ele.**

How much will you have to pay for this room?

Specifications

3 Getting value for money.
- **Está incluído o pequeno almoço?**
- □ **Sim, e o IVA também.**
(**também** = also)

What is included apart from breakfast?

Checking in

4 You have already made a reservation.
- **Mandei reservar.**
- □ **Qual é o seu nome, se faz favor?**
- **Chamo-me Gill Kirkpatrick.**
- □ **Ah, sim. Queira preencher esta ficha, se faz favor.**

The receptionist wants you to show your passport: true/false?

Services

5 Making sure you don't miss breakfast.
- **A que horas é o pequeno almoço?**
- □ **Das sete e meia às dez, e das oito às onze nos domingos.**

What is the latest time you can have breakfast on Sundays?

Problems

6 You are feeling the cold.
- **Há um problema com o aquecimento.**
- □ **Mando alguém.**

The receptionist says he will deal with it himself: true/false?

Checking out

7 At the desk
- **Queria pagar a conta.**
- □ **Qual é o número do seu quarto?**
- **Vinte e cinco.**
- □ **São doze mil escudos. Como vai pagar?**
- **Com cartão de crédito.**

How much is your hotel bill?

Campsites

8 You have just arrived at the site.
- **Tem lugar para um carro e uma caravana?**
- □ **Temos.**
- **Qual é o preço?**
- □ **São mil e duzentos escudos por dia para um carro e dois mil para uma caravana.**
(**Temos** = Yes, we have.)

How much more do they charge for the caravan?

Try it out

Matching

Match up the sentences in the first group with the responses of the second group.

1 **Tem um quarto duplo?**
2 **O duche não funciona.**
3 **Como vai pagar?**
4 **Onde é o bar?**
5 **A que horas é o pequeno almoço?**

a **Mando alguém.**
b **Com cartão de crédito.**
c **Das oito às dez e meia.**
d **Lamento, o hotel está cheio.**
e **É ao lado da loja.**

Crossword

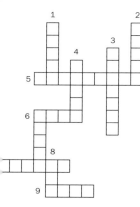

Across	Down
5 TV	1 shower
6 bed	2 car
8 window	3 swimming pool
9 nought	4 tent
	6 safe
	8 light

As if you were there

Going home.
■ (Say that you'd like to pay the bill)
□ **Qual é o número do seu quarto, se faz favor?**
■ (Your room number is: 8)
□ **Ah, sim . . . o senhor Smith. Como vai pagar?**
■ (Ask him how much it is)
□ **São nove mil escudos, senhor.**
■ (Tell him you'll pay by cash)
□ **Muito bom.**

Jumbled words

See if you can unravel these words. The clues should help you, but they are not in the right order!
Clues:
1 Your room's on the sixth floor, but there's the . . . to help you.
2 I'd like a room for two . . . and one child.
3 Can you help me? I have a . . . with the shower in my room.
4 I want to stay for one . . .
5 Would you mind letting me have your . . . please?

a **TENIO**
b **APEASPORTS**
c **REVELADO**
d **PRAMLOBE**
e **SADLOUT**

Sound Check

ch sounds like 'sh' in 'shed':
   duche (shower) sounds like 'doo-sher'
   chamo-me . . . (I'm called . . .) sounds like 'shar-moo mer'

nh sounds like 'ni' in 'onion':
   banho (bath) sounds like 'bar-nioo'
   dinheiro (money) sounds like 'di-niay-roo'

Buying things

Shops

Portugal is a relatively cheap country for locally produced goods such as clothes and ceramics, although imported food and electrical goods veer on the expensive side. Larger shops and supermarkets will accept major credit cards. If you pay cash, do not be surprised if change is rounded up – or down – to the nearest 5 escudos.

Shops are generally open from 9 am to 1 pm and 3 pm to 7 pm. Most close on Saturday afternoon and all day Sunday. However, larger supermarkets sometimes stay open seven days a week, often until midnight.

Towns also have at least one chemist open late night; check in the local paper or tourist office for details. These can supply most brands of medicines as well as contraceptives, sanitary towels and babies' nappies.

 How much is it?
Quanto custa?

Good-value goods

Shoes, usually well-crafted and of good-quality leather. Any shoe shop can offer bargains, such as those in the Baixa in Lisbon.

Clothes There is a large textiles industry in northern Portugal, with some companies supplying major international labels. Markets (see below) can sometimes throw up excellent-value seconds.

Ceramics and *azulejos* (tiles) Portuguese ceramics are distinctive and often beautifully decorative. Throughout Portugal, from resorts to the smallest village, there are stalls or shops selling ceramics and ornate tiles, while markets (see below) can also be a good source. Barcelos pottery – brown with yellow spots – is extremely popular. Look out for the cockerel motif which originated from a Barcelos legend and has become the symbol of Portuguese tourism.

Port and wine Port is excellent value and Portuguese wines are growing in reputation (see p70). Unless you happen to be passing a wine co-operative, your best bet is to stock up on these at the large supermarkets before you head home. Port tends to be cheaper in supermarkets than in Oporto's port lodges unless you want the top-quality stuff.

Olive oil This can be good value, either from supermarkets or from shops in the Alentejo or the Algarve where many of Portugal's olive groves are found.

Great markets

Most Portuguese towns have a weekly market, when people from the area congregate to buy and sell goods, be it livestock, clothes, crafts or locally grown food. They can be extremely lively and atmospheric and are worth a visit even if you do not intend to buy anything. In the not-to-be-missed category are:

Carcavelos market Half way along the train line from Lisbon to Cascais, this Thursday market is a huge, sprawling event where you can find some good ceramics and occasionally a bargain high-street label.

Feira da Ladra Lisbon's Tuesday and Saturday flea market, full of quirky cast-offs, clothes and music tapes.

Barcelos Portugal's biggest market occurs every Thursday in this attractive Minho town; its central square becomes crammed with everything from clothes and ceramics to live chickens and wooden barrels.

Viana do Castelo/Valença If you cannot make Barcelos, many of the stallholders rotate to the weekly markets in other Minho towns, such as on Fridays in Viana do Castelo, and Wednesdays in Valença.

Evas A Monday market when this cultured Alentejan town takes on an animated rural hue.

Portimão A characterful flea-market takes place in this Algarve town on the first Sunday of every month.

Can I try it on?
Posso experimentá-lo?

Buying food

Although buying food is not much cheaper than eating out at a restaurant, Portugal has some great fresh fish, fruit and vegetables and good-quality meat. Large supermarkets sell local and international produce, but if you are self-catering, or for a lunchtime picnic, the best place to buy supplies is from the town market. Even small towns have a covered market; go early to get the best buys. Prices should be displayed on the goods and it is not usual to bargain. Particularly good food markets include:

■ Mercado Bolhão, central Oporto.
■ Olhão harbourside market in the Algarve, particularly colourful and a great place to see a diverse range of fish.
■ Ribeira market, Lisbon, near Cais do Sodré.
■ Lavradores market, Funchal in Madeira.

Can I try some?
Posso provar?

Local goods

Other items which are good value in specific regions are:

■ **Ceramics** Try Barcelos in the Minho with its famous pottery; or the Coimbra region with its distinctive intricate animal motifs, just two of Portugal's many ceramics styles. Albufeira in the Algarve also has attractive pottery, while Estremoz in the Alentejo and Caldas da Rainha in Estremadura are famed for their earthenware.

■ **Metalwork** Go to Silves, Portimão or Loulé in the Algarve, a good place to buy the *cataplana* cooking pots from its metal workshops.

■ **Lace** Hand-made lace is produced in Loulé, Olhão and Castro Marim in the Algarve.

■ **Embroidery, rag quilts and bedspreads** Visit the Beira Baixa, especially Castelo Branco which is famed for its silk bedspreads, or Madeira, well known for its embroidery.

■ **Leather** Albufeira in the Algarve has good-quality leather goods, while Madeira specializes in leather boots.

■ **Tapestries** Go to the inland Alentejo, especially at Portalegre where some of its spectacular tapestries sell for hundreds of pounds; or to Madeira where tapestry is an ancient art.

■ **Carpets** Also in the Alentejo, visit Arraiolos, a small town north of Évora, the centre for some beautiful brightly coloured Persian-influenced carpets.

■ **Wickerwork baskets and cork mats** Two more finely crafted products from the Alentejo which make excellent gifts; wickerwork is also common in the Algarve and is the main trade in Camacha in Madeira.

■ **Filigree gold and silver** This is a speciality of the north and such products can make an attractive gift

Phrasemaker
Phrases to use anywhere

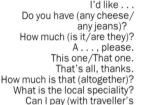

I'd like . . .	**Queria . . .**
Do you have (any cheese/any jeans)?	**Tem (queijo/jeans)?**
How much (is it/are they)?	**Quanto (custa/custam)?**
A . . . , please.	**Um/Uma . . . , se faz favor.**
This one/That one.	**Este/Aquele.**
That's all, thanks.	**Mais nada, obrigado/a.**
How much is that (altogether)?	**Quanto é (tudo) isso?**
What is the local speciality?	**Qual é a especialidade local?**
Can I pay (with traveller's cheques/by credit card)?	**Posso pagar com (traveller's cheques/cartão de crédito)?**

Que deseja?	What can I do for you?
Posso ajudá-lo?	Can I help you?
Lamento, não temos.	I'm sorry, we have none (left).
Aqui tem.	Here you are.
Mais alguma coisa?	Anything else?
É só?	Is that all?
É . . . (escudos) no total.	That's . . . (escudos) altogether.
Pague na caixa.	Pay at the cash desk.

STELARIA

Shops

English	Portuguese	English	Portuguese
antique shop	o antiquário	jeweller's	a joalharia
art gallery	a galeria de arte	laundry (dry cleaner's)	a lavanderia (a seco)
bookseller's	a livraria	market	o mercado
bread shop	a padaria	newsstand	o quiosque de jornais
butcher's	o talho	optician	o oculista
cake/pastry shop	a pastelaria	shoe shop	a sapataria
camera shop	a loja de artigos fotográficos	shop	a loja
chemist's	a farmácia	shopping centre	o centro comercial
clothes shop	a loja de roupas	souvenir shop	a loja de lembranças
dairy	a leitaria	sports shop	a loja de artigos desportivos
department store	o grande armazém	stationer's	a papelaria
fishmonger's	a peixaria	supermarket	o supermercado
florist's	a florista	tobacconist's	a tabacaria
food shop/grocer's	a mercearia	toy shop	a loja de brinquedos
hairdresser's	o cabeleireiro	wine merchant's	o comerciante de vinhos
hardware store	a loja de ferragens		
health food shop	a loja de produtos dietéticos		

61

Food shopping

How much (is it/are they) a kilo?	**Quanto (é/são) o quilo?**
a kilo of (apples/potatoes)	**um quilo de (maçãs/batatas)**
half a kilo of (cherries/flour)	**meio quilo de (cerejas/farina)**
100 grams of sweets	**cem gramas de rebuçados**
(See p33 for numbers.)	
a (bottle/tin/sachet) of . . .	**uma (garrafa/lata/saché) de . . .**
a (jar/packet) of . . .	**um (frasco/pacote) de . . .**
a slice of . . .	**uma fatia de . . .**
three slices of . . .	**três fatias de . . .**
Can I try (some/a piece)?	**Posso provar?**
A bit more/less, please.	**Um bocado mais/menos, se faz favor.**

Quanto quer?	How much would you like?
Quantos?	How many?
Qual?	Which one?
Temos vários tipos.	We have several types.

Containers/quantities

a kilo	**um quilo**	can/tin	**a lata**
half a kilo	**meio quilo**	jar	**o frasco**
100 grams	**cem gramas**	packet	**o pacote**
bottle	**a garrafa**	sachet	**o saché**

FECHADO

Buying clothes

I'm just looking, thank you.	**Estou só a ver, obrigado/a.**
I'd like a (shirt/pair of trousers).	**Queria (uma camisa/umas calças).**
I'm size 12.	**O meu número é doze.**
My English size is . . .	**O meu número inglês é . . .**
Can I try it on?	**Posso experimentá-lo (-la)?**
Can I try them on?	**Posso experimentá-los (-las)?**
They're a bit small.	**São um bocado pequenos/as.**
They're a bit big.	**São um bocado grandes.**
They're too narrow.	**São demasiado estreitos/as.**
. . . broad	**. . . largos/as**
Do you have anything (smaller/cheaper)?	**Tem mais (pequeno/barato)?**
Do you have the same in (yellow/green)?	**Tem isso em (amarelo/verde)?**
(See p35 for colours.)	
I like (it/them).	**Gosto.**
I don't like (it/them).	**Não gosto.**
It's very expensive.	**É muito caro.**
I'll take it.	**Fico com ele (ela).**
I'll take them.	**Fico com eles (elas).**
I'll think about it.	**Vou pensar.**

open

ABERTO

Que número?	What size are you?
Em que cor?	What colour?
O senhor/A senhora gosta (dele/dela/deles/delas)?	How do you like (it/them)?
Aquele (Aquela) é maior.	That one is bigger.

Department store

Where is the . . . department?	**Onde é a secção de . . . ?**
Where can I find (shoes/ladies' fashion)?	**Onde posso encontrar (sapatos/ moda de senhoras)?**
Is there a lift?	**Há ascensor?**
rés-do-chão.	
on the ground floor.	
(primeiro/segundo) andar.	
on the (first/second) floor.	

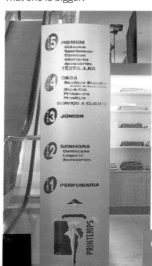

63

Correio Az

última hora 19:00

Buying stamps

How much is a stamp for (England/the USA)?	**Quanto é um selo para mandar (à Inglaterra/ aos Estados Unidos)?**
for a (letter/postcard)	**para (uma carta/um postal)**
Two . . . escudos stamps, please.	**Dois selos de . . . escudos, se faz favor.**
I'd like to send this to (Australia/Austria).	**Queria mandar isto a (Austrália/Áustria).**

Photography

a 35-mm film for (prints/slides)	**um rolo de trinta e cinco milímetr para (fotografias/slides)**
batteries	**as pilhas**
Can you develop this?	**Pode revelar isto?**
When will it be ready?	**Quando estará pronto?**

hoje	today
amanhã	tomorrow
daqui a (uma hora/três horas)	in (1 hour/3 hours)

Fruit and nuts

apples	**as maçãs**	oranges	**as laranjas**
apricots	**os alperces**	peaches	**os pêssegos**
bananas	**as bananas**	peanuts	**os amendoins**
cherries	**as cerejas**	pears	**as pêras**
chestnuts	**as castanhas**	pineapple	**o ananás**
dates	**as tâmaras**	plums	**as ameixas**
figs	**os figos**	raspberries	**as framboesas**
grapefruit	**a toranja**	strawberries	**os morangos**
grapes	**as uvas**	sultanas/	**as passas**
hazelnuts	**as avelãs**	raisins	
lemon/lemons	**o limão/os limões**	walnuts	**as nozes**
melon	**o melão**	watermelon	**a melancia**

Vegetables

asparagus	**os espargos**	lettuce	**a alface**
aubergine	**a berinjela**	mushroom	**o cogumelo**
beans, broad	**as favas**	onions	**as cebolas**
beans, green	**os feijões, as**	parsley	**a salsa**
	vagens	peas	**as ervilhas**
cabbage, white	**o repolho**	peppers	**os pimentos**
carrots	**as cenouras**	(capsicum)	
cauliflower	**a couve-flor**	potatoes	**as batatas**
chick peas	**os grãos**	(boiled)	**(cozidas)**
cucumber	**o pepino**	radishes	**os rabanetes**
garlic	**o alho**	spinach	**o(s) espina-**
kale	**a couve por-**		**fre(s)**
	tuguesa	sweetcorn	**o milho**
lentils	**as lentilhas**	tomatoes	**os tomates**

(See also Menu reader p85)

Supermarket

bread	**o pão**	mineral water	**a água mineral**
cheese	**o queijo**	(fizzy/	**(com gás/**
coffee	**o café**	still)	**sem gás)**
cold meat	**as carnes frias**	sardines, tin	**a lata de**
detergent (for	**o detergente**		**sardinhas**
clothes)	**para roupa**	spicy	**o chouriço**
ham	**o presunto**	sausage	
honey	**o mel**	tea	**o chá**
lemonade	**a limonada**	washing-up	**o detergente**
milk	**o leite**	liquid	**para louça**

Specialities

o chouriço	spicy pork sausage, made with paprika	**os papo-secos/ pãezinhos**	bread rolls
		o presunto	cured ham
		as queijadas	cheesecakes

Newsagent's/stationer's

batteries	**as pilhas**	newspapers,	**os jornais**
cigarettes	**os cigarros**	English	**ingleses**
envelopes	**os envelopes**	paper	**o papel**
film	**o rolo**	pen	**a caneta**
guidebook	**o guia**	pencil	**o lápis**
magazines	**as revistas**	postcard	**o postal**
map of the city	**a planta da**	stamps	**os selos**
	cidade	sweets	**os rebuçados**
matches	**os fósforos**	telephone card	**o cartão de**
			telefone

Toiletries

brush	a escova	tissues	os lenços de papel
comb	o pente	toilet paper	o papel higié-nico
deodorant	o desodorizante	toothbrush	a escova de dentes
razor blades	as lâminas de barbear	toothpaste	a pasta de dentes
sanitary towels	os pensos higiénicos		
shampoo	o shampoo		
soap	o sabonete		

Clothes and materials

belt	o cinto	shoes	os sapatos
blouse	a blusa	shorts	os calções
bra	o soutien	skirt	a saia
coat	o casaco	socks	as peúgas
dress	o vestido	sunglasses	os óculos de s
gloves	as luvas	sweater	a camisola
handbag	o saco de mão	swimming costume	o fato de banh
hat	o chapéu	T-shirt	o T-shirt
jacket	o casaco	tie	a gravata
jeans	os jeans	tights	o collant
pullover	o pulôver	tracksuit	o fato de trein
raincoat	o impermeável	trousers	as calças
sandals	as sandálias	underpants	as cuecas
scarf	o cachecol		
shirt	a camisa		

Souvenirs: national specialities

os artigos de (cabedal/couro/pele)	leather articles	o galo de Barcelos	the Barcelos cockerel
		os lenços	handkerchief
os artigos de madeira	woodwork	as louças de barro	earthenware
os artigos de verga	wickerwork	as louças de porcelana	china
os azulejos	tiles	as rendas	lacework
os bordados	embroidery	os tapetes	rugs
a cataplana	a type of cooking pot	os xailes	shawls
as filigranas	filigree jewellery		

Language works

Food shopping

You want to buy some ham and some cheese.

Bom dia, queria meio quilo de presunto, se faz favor.
Com certeza. Mais alguma coisa?
Duzentas gramas de queijo.
Temos muitos tipos. Qual prefere?
Posso provar este?
Pode . . . Gosta?
Gosto, sim. Queria meio quilo, se faz favor.
Com certeza = Certainly; **Qual prefere?** = Which do you prefer?)

Why does he let you try some cheese?

Buying clothes

You want to buy a T-shirt.
Posso ajudá-lo?
Gosto desta T-shirt.
Que número?
O meu número é quarenta e um.
Esta é muito pequena. Aquela é maior.
Posso experimentá-la?
Pode. Vem por aqui, se faz favor.
Vem por aqui = Come this way)

Were you able to try it on?

Buying stamps

3 You want to buy some stamps.
- **Vendem selos?**
- **Quantos quer?**
- **Queria quatro selos para Inglaterra.**
- **São cento e vinte escudos.**

How much will you have to pay?

Souvenirs

4 You want a special present to take home.
- **Bom dia. Qual é a especialidade local?**
- **Temos filigranas, louças de barro, azulejos e xailes.**
- **Gosto deste xaile. Quanto é?**
- **Cinco mil escudos.**
- **É muito caro. Posso pagar com cartão de crédito?**

Why did you want to pay by credit card?

Newsagent's

5 You want to read an English paper.
- **Tem jornais ingleses?**
- **Temos. À esquerda.**

The papers are on the . . .

Try it out

Shopping list

See if you can unravel the words on this shopping list.
1 uma *taal* de *shandrais*
2 cem *smagra* de *joique*
3 uma *farraga* de água *lermina*
4 meio *liquo* de *sounterp*
5 um *trilo* de *hinov*

Crossword

¹					
	■		■		
²		³		⁴	
	■		■		
	■		■		
⁵					

Across
1 shoe
2 shirt
5 handbag (with 1 and 3 down)

Down
1 and 3 handbag (with 5 across)
4 skirt

As if you were there

You are trying on some shoes in a shoe shop.
■ (Say that you want to try on some shoes)

□ **Com certeza. Qual é o seu número?**
■ (Say that your English size is 6)
□ **O seu número continental é trinta e nove. Em que côr?**
■ (Say 'black')
After trying on several pairs, you decide on the pair you like best
□ (Say that you'll take them)

Opposites

Find the opposites for these words.
1 **grande**
2 **estreito**
3 **barato**

Sound Check

x sounds like 'sh' in 'shed':
   caixa (cash desk) sounds like '**ky**-sher'
   peixaria (fishmonger's) sounds like 'pay-sher-**ree**-er'

lh sounds like 'lli' in 'million':
   talho (butcher's) sounds like '**tar**-llioo'
   pilhas (batteries) sounds like '**pee**-lliersh'

Café life

Busy times in cafés and *pastelarias* (patisseries) include breakfast (around 7 till 9 am), when many Portuguese have a quick pastry or toast and coffee, and tea (4 till 5 pm), when Portuguese pastries and cakes come into their own.

What snacks do you have?
Que refeições leves tem?

Where to eat

Pastelarias are your best bet for breakfast and tea, usually offering a fine range of croissants, pastries, cakes, tea and coffee. Don't miss *pastéis de nata*, custard tarts traditionally made in Belém: best when fresh and dusted with cinnamon, they make the perfect tea-time snack. Many *pastelarias* also offer light lunch possibilities such as *pastéis de bacalhau* (fishcakes), *pastéis de carne* (meat pies) and *sandes* (sandwiches).

Cafés offer a similar range of goodies for breakfast or for a lunch of soups, *tostas* (toasted sandwiches), *bifanas* or *pregos* (grilled pork or steak rolls or sandwiches). Larger cafés and *tascas* (taverns) serve full set lunches.

Is there a toilet?
Há casa de banho?

Wines, drinks and spirits to sample

Port *Vinho do Porto* is fortified wine, perhaps Portugal's most famous drink. Try a cool *porto branco* (white port) as an aperitif.

Vinho verde These light, young wines are extremely tasty and refreshing, though the white is more accessible than the red.

Vinho maduro Mature Portuguese wines are growing in reputation internationally, and almost every region has a fine local wine. Some of the best wine regions include Dão, Douro, Bairrada, and Colares.

Moscatel A sweet, fruity dessert wine from just south of Lisbon.

Madeira Cool fortified wine; try the sweet Malmsey and Bual, the medium Verdelho or the dry Sercial.

Sagres beer A thirst-quenching lager, although in northern Portugal Superbock is the more common *cerveja* (beer). If you want draught beer, ask for *uma caneca* or *uma imperial* (*um fino* in the north).

Macieira One of the smoothest of Portugal's potent *aguardentes* (brandies), a good drink to round off a meal.

Ginginha A cherry liqueur, which comes 'with or without the stone'; bars specializing in this liqueur tend to be very popular.

Bica A wickedly strong espresso coffee, guaranteed to perk you up; a must for most Portuguese in the mornings.

Galão A milky coffee served in a tall glass, good for accompanying local pastries.

Chá com limão Tea with lemon, a refreshing drink best had in one of Portugal's many *salões de chá* (tea rooms).

❗ Do you have any soft drinks, please?
● **Há refrigerantes, se faz favor?**

Phrasemaker

Signs

café	café: for a large range of snacks
cervejaria	large café serving beer and shellfish
confeitaria	cake shop
pastelaria	patisserie
pequeno almoço	breakfast
pré-pagamento	payment in advance
salão de chá	tea room
tasca	tavern

prego

Asking what there is

Do you have (sandwiches/orange juice)?	**Tem (sandes/sumo de laranja)?**
What (snacks/sandwiches/cakes) do you have?	**Que (refeições leves/sandes/bolos) tem?**
Do you have any soft drinks, please?	**Há refrigerantes, se faz favor?**
Can I see what you have?	**Pode-se ver o que tem?**
What do you recommend?	**O que recomenda?**
Faz favor?	Can I help you?
O que deseja (comer/beber)?	What would you like to (eat/drink)?
Lamento, não temos.	I'm sorry, we haven't any.
Só temos . . .	We only have . . .

Ordering

I'd like . . .	**Queria . . .**
I'll take this.	**Quero isto.**
I'd like to try . . .	**Queria provar . . .**
a portion of . . .	**uma dose de . . .**
Waiter! Another beer!	**Se faz favor! Mais uma cerveja!**
How much is it, please?	**Quanto é, se faz favor?**

Grande ou pequeno?	Large or small?
Temos . . .	We have . . .
Fresco ou natural?	Ice cold or room temperature?
. . . com gelo?	. . . with ice?
Mais alguma coisa?	Anything else?
Que sabor?	Which flavour?
Qual?	Which one?
É self-service.	It's self-service.

Other useful phrases

Here you are.	**Aqui está.**
Do you have any change?	**Tem troco?**
Where are the toilets?	**Onde são as casas de banho?**
Is there a telephone?	**Há telefone?**

lá no fundo	over there at the back
à (direita/esquerda)	on the (right/left)
lá em (cima/baixo)	upstairs/downstairs
ao pé da porta	next to the door

Signs

Homens	Men's toilet
Senhoras	Ladies' toilet
Telefone	Telephone

HOMENS

SENHORAS

Containers/quantities

glass	**o copo**	can	**a lata**
bottle	**a garrafa**	carafe/jug	**o jarro**

Soft drinks

cola	**a cola**	ice cold/	**fresca/**
fruit juice	**o sumo de fruta**	room	**natural)**
grape juice	**o sumo de uva**	temperature)	
lemonade	**a limonada**	orange juice	**o sumo de**
milk	**o leite**		**laranja**
milkshake	**o batido**	orangeade	**a laranjada**
mineral	**a água mineral**	peach juice	**o sumo de**
water,	**(com gás/**		**pêssego**
(fizzy/still/	**sem gás/**	pineapple juice	**o sumo de**
			ananás

Alcoholic drinks

beer/lager	**a cerveja**	port	**o vinho do Porto**
beer, draught	**a imperial/**	whisky	**o uísque**
	a caneca/	wine	**o vinho**
	o fino (in the	(red/white)	**o vinho (tinto/**
	north)	wine	**branco)**
beer, bottled	**a garrafa de**	Madeira wine	**o vinho da**
	cerveja		**Madeira**
brandy	**o aguardente**	(dry/sweet)	**o vinho (seco/**
cognac	**o conhaque**	wine	**doce)**
gin and tonic	**o gin-tónico**	with ice	**com gelo**

Hot drinks

black coffee (very strong)	**a bica/o café**
coffee	**o café**
decaffeinated coffee	**o café descafeinado**
hot chocolate	**o chocolate quente**
tea	**o chá**
tea with (milk/lemon)	**o chá com (leite/limão)**
white coffee	**o café com leite/o garoto**
white coffee (large, milky)	**o galão**

Savoury snacks

beef sandwich/roll	**o prego**
cheese sandwich	**a sandes de queijo**
chips	**as batatas fritas**
fried egg and chips	**o ovo estrelado e batatas fritas**
ham sandwich	**a sandes de fiambre**
hamburger	**o hambúrguer**
hot dog	**o cachorro (quente)**
pork roll	**a bifana**
sandwich	**a sandes**
steak sandwich	**o prego**
toast	**a torrada**
toasted cheese and ham sandwich	**a tosta mixta**
toasted sandwich	**a tosta**

Typical Portuguese snacks

os acepipes variados	assorted appetizers (hors-d'œuvres)
as azeitonas (recheadas)	(stuffed) olives
os camarões	shrimps
as carnes frias	cold meats
o chouriço	spicy red sausage
. . . de peixe	. . . made with fish
as lulas grelhadas	grilled squid
o melão com presunto	melon with ham
os pastéis de (bacalhau/ carne)	(fish/meat) pasties
os rissóis	fried pasties with various fillings
as sardinhas	sardines

o croissant	croissant	**a queijada**	cheese tart
o bolo	cake	**os bolinhos de amêndoa**	almond biscuits
o pastel de nata/de Belém	custard tart		

Ice-creams

What flavours do you have?	**Que sabores tem?**
ice-cream	**o gelado**
apricot	**alperce**
chocolate	**chocolate**
coffee	**café**
pistachio	**pistache**
strawberry	**morango**
vanilla	**baunilha**

Language works

Asking what there is

1 You want a sandwich.
☐ **O que deseja?**
■ **Tem sandes?**
☐ **Lamento, não temos.**

Do they have any sandwiches? Yes or no?

2 You missed breakfast at the hotel and go to a café.
■ **Tem pequeno almoço?**
☐ **Sim, senhora. Temos bolos e torradas.**
■ **Uma torrada, se faz favor.**
☐ **O que deseja beber?**

At the end, does the waiter ask (a) what you want to eat or (b) what you want to drink?

3 You are feeling adventurous and want to try something typical.
■ **Que petiscos tem?**
☐ **Temos rissóis de peixe, pregos e sardinhas.**

Do all the snacks contain fish? Yes or no?

Ordering

4 A sweet tooth?
■ **Queria um chá com leite e um garoto.**
☐ **São cento e cinquenta escudos. Mais alguma coisa?**
■ **Queria provar dois pastéis de nata. Quanto custam?**
☐ **São duzentos e setenta escudos.**

How much was the total bill?

5 Your favourite ice-cream flavour is strawberry.
■ **Um gelado de morango, se faz favor.**
☐ **Lamento. Só temos de baunilha.**

What flavour are you offered?

Try it out

Find the word

Use the clue to unravel these words
1 cold breakfast drink
   u daft mouser
2 sounds cold, but refreshing
   grins at reefer
3 icy dessert
   dolage
4 milky drink
   itodab
5 more than just a piece of bread
   toast
6 breakfast cup
   ragoot
7 beefy snack
   grope
8 fruit of the summer
   gramono
9 lunchtime snack
   sneads

pasteis de Belém

As if you were there

Time for an aperitif
- (Call the waiter and ask for a gin and tonic)
- □ **Com gelo?**
- (Say 'yes' and order a white wine as well)
- □ **Mais alguma coisa? Azeitonas?**
- (Say you want to try some assorted appetizers)
- □ **Em seguida, senhor.**

(**Em seguida** = Straight away)

Downword

Fill in the items going down and you'll be able to work out the edible treat across the top.

1 Perhaps the most popular ice cream flavour.
2 Nearly always in your pocket or purse.
3 Have we? Yes!
4 Opposite of 'com'.
5 Those tasty filled pasties.
6 A complement to gin. Sounds good for you!
7 Strawberry, vanilla and pistachio are all . . . of ice cream.

	1		2		3		4		5		6		7	
	A		A		A		F		I		A			

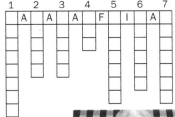

acepipes variados

Sound Check

z is pronounced in two different ways: it usually sounds like 'z' in 'zoo', but at the end of a word it sounds like 'sh' in 'shed':
 faz favor (please) sounds like 'fersh fer-**voar**'
 azeitonas (olives) sounds like 'er-zay-**toh**-nersh'

Ways of pronouncing **e**.

If it's not stressed, it sounds like 'er' or 'a' in 'asleep'; if it is stressed, it sounds like 'eh' or 'e' in 'pet':
 pequeno (little) sounds like 'per-**keh**-noo'

If it's before an 'i', the 'e' and 'i' together make the sound 'ay', and at the end of a word it's often not pronounced:
 leite (milk) sounds like 'layt'

Before 'm' it makes the nasal sound:
 tem (you have) sounds like '**tay**' but through the nose.

At the beginning of a word it sounds like 'i' in 'hit':
 está (he is) sounds like 'ish-**tar**'

é sounds like 'eh' or 'e' in 'egg':
 café sounds like 'ker-**feh**'

ê sounds like 'a' in 'hay':
 você sounds like 'voo-**say**'

Eating out

Meal times

Most Portuguese eat out frequently, mainly because it can often be as cheap to eat at a restaurant as it to cook the same meal at home. Lunchtime *pratos do dia* (specials) are particularly cheap, and most restaurants will be packed during work lunchbreaks (around 12 till pm). Restaurant meals out during the evenings (around 8 till 10 pm, later in summer resorts) and weekends are slightly more expensive, although the *ementa turística* (set meal of the day) is good value. Restaurant meals tend to be family affairs; do not be surprised to see children out and about until midnight.

What do you recommend?
O que recomenda?

Vegetarian options

Complete vegetarians have a hard time in standard restaurants and may be limited to starter or side options such as vegetable soup, omelette or salads.

Where to eat

Restaurants are your best bet for a full evening meal, along with *cervejarias* (large places often selling seafood and good beers) or *churrasqueiras* (specializing in grilled or barbecued food). *Marisqueiras* (specializing in seafood) tend to be marginally more expensive.
Cafés see p69.
Fast food The main towns and resorts now have a growing number of fast-food chains; ironically this convenience food tends to be more expensive than dishes at local restaurants.

I'd like the set menu, please.
Queria a ementa turística.

Types of food

Being an Atlantic country, fish and seafood are usually of good quality. Most restaurants will have a fine local fresh fish, *bacalhau* (salted cod) or seafood dish, whilst pork and chicken are reliable staples for meat eaters. Beef, lamb, goat, rabbit, suckling pig and even wild boar are also fairly common. Portuguese food tends to be cooked with plenty of olive oil, garlic and coriander, although sauces and accompanying vegetables are a rare feature.

bacalhau à Gomez de Sá

**What's the local speciality?
Qual é a especialidade da região?**

If you are in the region, try these local specialities:

Oporto and the Douro *Tripas à moda do Porto* (tripe with beans); *cação em vinho tinto* (a thick fish stew in a red wine sauce).

Minho *Truta* (fresh river trout, often grilled with a thick slice of *presunto* inside); *lombo de porco assado* (roast pork loin); *fatias de Braga* (a sweet almond cake).

Trás-os-Montes *Sopa de castanha* (chestnut soup); *feijoada* (meat and bean stew); *nogado* (nut and honey nougat).

Beira Alta *Queijo da serra* (a mountain cheese); *chouriço* (a spicy sausage); *fios* (a Moorish sweetmeat, meaning 'threads').

Beira Baixa *cabrito assado* (roast kid).

Coimbra and Beira Litoral *Sopa de caldeirada* (mixed fish soup); *leitão assado* (roast suckling pig).

Lisbon and Estremadura *Lulas fritas* (fried fresh squid); *iscas* (marinated liver cooked with *presunto* and potatoes); *santola recheada* (stuffed spider crab); *queijadas* (cheesecakes from Sintra).

Ribatejo *Favas à ribatejana* (broad bean and pork stew); *pudim de cenoura* (carrot pudding).

Alentejo *Açorda* (a bread-and-garlic-based white sauce to accompany other dishes); *lulas recheadas* (stuffed squid); *cerieaia com ameixas* (sponge cake with plum sauce), cheeses from Nisa.

Algarve *Sardinhas no churrasco*

sardinhas no churrasco

(barbecued sardines); *cataplana de amêijoas* (clam stew); *bolos de Dom Rodrigo* (an egg sweet made with almonds and syrup); *brandymel*, a honey-brandy.

Madeira *Bife de atum e milho frito* (tuna steaks with fried maize); *carne de vinhos e alhos* (fried pork marinated in wine, garlic and spices); *bolo de mel* (honey cake); *maracujá* (passionfruit juice).

**The bill, please.
A conta, se faz favor.**

Phrasemaker

Is there a good restaurant near here?

Há um bom restaurante perto daqui?

O CHAFARIZ

COSTELINHAS à CHAFARIZ
PATO NO FORNO C/ARROZ
PATANISCAS C/ARROZ FEIJÃO
BACALHAU À CASA
PEIXE FRESCO DO DIA
FEIJOADA DE MARISCO
=3500.00 -2 PESSOAS =
ARROZ DE MARISCO
=3500.00 - 2 PESSOAS=
DESCANSO DO PESSOAL
SEGUNDAS-FEIRAS

CHURRASQUEIRA
O FORNO
◄ a 50 Metros

Places to eat

o café	for a range of snacks
a casa de fados	restaurant where you will hear the traditional Portuguese **fado** music
a cervejaria	large café serving beer and shellfish
a confeitaria	cake shop
a churrasqueira	large café specializing in grilled or barbecued food
a marisqueira	shellfish and seafood restaurant
a pastelaria	patisserie
o restaurante	restaurant
o salão de chá	tea room
o snack-bar	snack bar
a tasca	tavern

MARISQUEIRA

ESPECIALIDAD
GRELHADOS
PEIXES FRESCOS | CARNE
BACALHAU | DE NOVI
LINGUADO | COSTEL
SALMONETE | ESPETA
CHERNE | BIFE
PEIXE ESPADA | DE POR
CHOCOS | ENTREC
LULAS | COSTEL
CARAPAUS | FEBRAS
SARDINHAS | DE BOM
| ESPETA
FRANCO NO CHURR.
◄MARISCOS►
CAMARÃO
COZIDO E GRELHA

Arriving

A table for (two/four) people	**Uma mesa para (duas/quatro) pessoas**
(See p35 for days of the week and p33 for clock times.)	
Do you have a table now?	**Tem uma mesa agora?**
I have booked a table for three.	**Tenho uma mesa reservada para três pessoas.**
Can we eat outside?	**Pode-se comer lá fora?**
. . . near the window?	**. . . perto da janela?**
. . . away from the door?	**. . . longe da porta?**
. . . in a non-smoking area?	**. . . numa zona para não-fumadores?**
Qual é o seu nome?	What is your name?
Para quantas pessoas?	For how many people?
A que horas?	At what time?
Lamento, não temos mesa.	I'm sorry, we don't have a table.
Pode esperar uns vinte minutos?	Can you wait for about 20 minutes?
Queria sentar-se aqui?	Would you like to sit here?
Queria tomar (uma bebida/um aperitivo)?	Would you like to have (a drink/ an aperitif)?
Queria pedir agora?	Would you like to order now?

Asking about the menu

The menu, please.	**A ementa, se faz favor.**
Have you got (a set menu)?	**Tem (ementa turística)?**
Does that include (bread/wine)?	**Inclui (pão/vinho)?**
What is the dish of the day?	**Qual é o prato do dia?**
What do you recommend?	**O que recomenda?**
What's the local speciality?	**Qual é a especialidade da região?**
Is service included?	**Está incluído o serviço?**

Ordering

I'd like . . .	**Queria . . .**
. . . for first course . . .	**. . . para o primeiro prato . . .**
. . . for the main course . . .	**. . . para o prato principal . . .**
. . . for dessert . . .	**. . . para a sobremesa . . .**
Can you tell me what . . . is?	**Pode dizer-me o que é . . . ?**
I'd like a half-portion of . . .	**Queria meia dose de . . .**

lulas fritas

O que deseja?	What would you like?
Hoje temos . . .	Today we have . . .
Recomendamos . . .	We recommend . . .
Para beber?	To drink?
Quer sobremesa?	Would you like a dessert?
Lamento, só temos . . .	I'm sorry, we only have . . .
É (um peixe grande e branco/ um tipo de cebola).	It's (a large white fish/a kind of onion).
Bom apetite!	Enjoy your meal!
Como deseja a carne?	How would you like your meat?

Eating habits

I can't eat . . .	**Não posso comer . . .**
What is in the sauce?	**Como é o molho?**
I'm allergic to . . .	**Sou alérgico/a a . . .**
I'm vegetarian	**Sou vegetariano/a**
Does it contain . . .?	**Contém . . .?**

arroz de marisco

Drinks

Is there a wine list?	**Há uma lista dos vinhos?**
a (bottle/half-bottle) of (red/ white/rosé) wine	**(uma garrafa/meia garrafa) de vinho (tinto/branco/rosado)**
a beer	**uma cerveja**
I'd like to try . . .	**Queria provar . . .**
(fizzy/still) mineral water	**água mineral (com gás/sem gás)**
tap water	**água da torneira**

At your table

ashtray	**o cinzeiro**		salt	**o sal**
bottle	**a garrafa**		saucer	**o pires**
bowl	**a tigela**		spoon	**o colher**
chair	**a cadeira**		sugar	**o açúcar**
cup	**a chávena**		table	**a mesa**
fork	**o garfo**		tablecloth	**a toalha de mesa**
glass	**o copo**		teaspoon	**o colher de chá, a colherzinha**
knife	**a faca**			
napkin	**o guardanapo**		toothpicks	**os palitos**
oil	**o azeite**		vinegar	**o vinagre**
pepper	**a pimenta**			
plate	**o prato**			

guardanapo

During the meal

Excuse me!/Waiter!	**Se faz favor!**
I didn't order . . .	**Não pedi . . .**
Another (bottle of) . . .	**Mais (uma garrafa de) . . .**
More bread, please.	**Mais pão, se faz favor.**
It's (cold/underdone).	**Está (frio/mal passado).**
The knife is dirty.	**A faca está suja.**
Could you bring me . . .?	**Pode trazer-me . . .?**
It's very good!	**Está muito bom!**
Nothing else, thanks.	**Mais nada, obrigado/a.**
Where are the toilets?	**Onde é a casa de banho?**
Is smoking allowed?	**Pode-se fumar?**

Para quem é (o bife/a salada)?	Who is the (steak/salad) for?
Está tudo bem?	Is everything all right?
Como está o . . .?	How's the . . . ?
Mais alguma coisa?	Anything else?

Paying

The bill, please.	**A conta, se faz favor.**
Is service included?	**Está incluído o serviço?**
Is there a mistake here?	**A conta está certa aqui?**
We didn't have (any beer/ a dessert).	**Não tomámos (cerveja/ sobremesa).**
Do you accept credit cards?	**Aceita cartões de crédito?**

Language works

Setting a table

Any room?
Tem uma mesa para quatro pessoas?
Pode esperar uns dez minutos?

You'll only have to wait for . . . minutes.

Enjoying the view.
Pode-se comer lá fora?
Lamento, não temos mesa lá fora. Queria sentar-se perto da janela?

You may still be able to see the view: true/false?

Ordering

You are looking for a cheap lunch.
Qual é o prato do dia?
Frango com batatas fritas.
Inclui vinho?
Sim, inclui uma garrafa de vinho.

What is the main meal, fish, chicken, veal or pork? What is included with the meal?

What's in the stew?
O que me recomenda?
Recomendamos a caldeirada.
Pode dizer-me o que é?
Peixe com cebola, tomate e batatas.

The dish he recommends includes fish and potatoes: true/false?

Drink

5 Trying something new.
■ **Queria provar um vinho branco. Tem doce?**
□ **Lamento, só temos vinho branco seco.**
■ **Está bem.**

What kind of white wine do you settle for?

During the meal

6 You need some assistance.
■ **Onde é a casa de banho?**
□ **A casa de banho é perto da porta, senhor.**

Where is the toilet: outside, near the window or near the door?

Paying

7 You can't read the bill.
■ **A conta está certa aqui?**
□ **Não, senhor. É dois mil e duzentos escudos.**
■ **O serviço está incluído?**
□ **Está incluído, senhor.**

How much is the total bill?

carne de porco à Alentejana

83

Try it out

Crossword

Across
4 Protect yourself from spills.
5 (and 4 down) Attack your main course with these!
9 Draught or bottled.

Down
1 Wine.
2 Essential for drinking wine.
3 (and 7) Season your food.
6 Use this to enjoy your soup with.
8 What the food is served on.

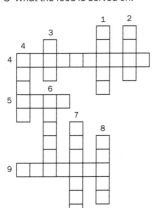

Matching halves

Here are twelve halves of words. Match them up to find six things that you will find in a restaurant (not necessarily to eat or drink).

ME	LAS	TA	LU	MOL	SO
PA	HO	CAR	SA	NE	POR

The right course

Match the food item with the right course. All these words are jumbled up. Unscramble them and then put the food into the correct course (menu heading).

Food	Menu heading
ROGBERO	**SPACEPIE**
SHALIVER	**VASE**
STOANEZIA	**CRAMSISO**
GAFORN	**CANER**
SAMBAG	**GLUMEES**

Sound Check

More practice with nasal sounds
   sal<u>ão</u>, amanh<u>ã</u>, <u>um</u>, s<u>em</u>, cont<u>ém</u>

q is always followed by 'u'. It is said in two different ways.
When **qu** is followed by 'a' it sounds like 'qua' in 'quack':
   quatro (four) sounds like 'kwar-troo'

When **qu** is followed by 'e' it sounds like 'k' in 'keen':
   queria (I'd like) sounds like 'ker-**ree**-er'

santola

Menu reader

The courses

aperitivos e acepipes/ entradas/petiscos	starters
sopas	soups
saladas	salads
prato principal/segundo prato	main course
peixes	fish
mariscos	shellfish
carne	meat
aves	poultry
caça	game
legumes	vegetables
sobremesas/doces	desserts
fruta	fruit

Main ways of cooking

à cataplana	cooked in a round copper pan with a tight-fitting lid
assado	roast
bem passado	well done
cozido	boiled
cozido ao vapor	steamed
escaldado	poached
frito	fried
fumado	smoked
grelhado	grilled
mal passado	rare, underdone
marinado	marinated
médio passado	medium done
no churrasco	barbecued
no forno	in the oven, baked

The menu

acepipes starters
   variados assorted appetizers
açorda thick bread-and-garlic-based soup
   de marisco thick bread soup with seafood
   à Alentejana thick bread soup with garlic and herbs
açúcar sugar
alho garlic
alperces apricots
amêijoas clams
ameixas plums
amêndoas almonds
amendoins peanuts
ananás pineapple
anchovas anchovies
aperitivos aperitifs
arroz rice
   doce rice pudding
   de frango chicken with rice
   de marisco seafood rice
   de manteiga rice with butter
   e massa rice and pasta
atum tuna, tunny
avelãs hazelnuts
aves poultry
azeite oil

azeitonas olives
   recheadas stuffed olives
   pretas black olives
bacalhau cod
   à Brás cod with eggs and potatoes
   à Gomes de Sá cod with black olives, garlic, onions and potatoes
banana banana
batatas potatoes
   fritas chips
   cozidas boiled potatoes
baunilha vanilla
berinjela aubergine
bife steak (ie the cut)
   de atum tuna steak
   de porco pork steak
   de vaca beef steak
bolinhos de amêndoa almond biscuits
bolos cakes
borrego lamb
cabrito kid
caça game
cação em vinho tinto fish stew in red wine sauce
café coffee
caldeirada fish stew
caldo verde soup made from shredded kale, with potato and spicy sausage
camarões shrimps
canja de galinha chicken soup
caracóis snails
caranguejo crab
carne meat
   de porco à Alentejana pork with clams
carnes frias cold meats
castanhas chestnuts
cataplana round, copper pan with tight-fitting lid
cavala mackerel
cebolas onions
cenouras carrots
cerejas cherries
chocolate chocolate
chocos cuttlefish

com tinta cuttlefish in its ink
chouriço spicy pork sausage, with paprika and garlic
codorniz quail
coelho rabbit
cogumelo mushroom
costeletas chops
couve portuguesa kale
couve-flor cauliflower
cozido à Portuguesa stew with beef, bacon, sausage and vegetables
doces desserts
enguia eel
entradas starters
ervilhas peas
espadarte swordfish
espargos asparagus
esparguete spaghetti
espetadas kebabs
faisão pheasant
fatias de Braga sweet almond cake
favas broad beans
feijão verde green beans
feijoada meat and bean stew
fígado com arroz liver with rice
figos figs
fios Moorish sweetmeat
framboesas raspberries
frango chicken

na púcura chicken stewed in port, then fried with wine and almonds
fruta fruit
galinha boiling fowl
gambas king prawns
gaspacho à Alentejana chilled soup with tomatoes, cucumbers, peppers and onions
gelado ice-cream
grão chick peas
iscas (à Portuguesa) liver (marinated in wine and garlic, then fried)
javali wild boar
laranja orange
lebre hare
legumes vegetables
leitão sucking pig
lentilhas lentils
limão lemon

frango

linguado sole
lombo loin of pork
lulas squid
maçã apple
macarrão macaroni
mariscos shellfish
marmelada quince jelly
massa pasta
mel honey
melancia watermelon
melão melon
   com presunto melon with ham
mexilhões mussels
migas de bacalhau dried cod soup with garlic
milho sweetcorn
molho sauce
morangos strawberries
mousse de chocolate chocolate mousse
nogado nougat
nozes walnuts
omeleta omelette
ostras oysters
ovos eggs
   cozidos boiled eggs
   estrelados fried eggs
   mexidos scrambled eggs

passas sultanas, raisins
pastel de nata/de Belém custard tart
pastelaria pastries
pato duck
peixes fish
pepino cucumber
pêra pear
perdiz partridge
peru turkey
pescada hake
pêssego peach
petiscos snacks, starters
pimenta pepper
pimentos peppers, capsicum
   assados roast peppers
pistacho pistachio
polvo octopus
porco pork
prato principal main course
presunto cured ham
pudim flan crème caramel
queijada cheesecake
queijo cheese
rabanetes radishes
repolho white cabbage
rins kidneys
rissóis rissoles

javali

robalo   sea-bass
sal   salt
salada   salad
  de atum   tuna fish salad
  de feijão   salad with black
  beans
  de tomate   tomato salad
  de alface   lettuce salad
  mista   side salad
  russa   salad with diced
  vegetables and mayonnaise
salmão   salmon
santola   spider crab
sardinhas   sardines
segundo prato   main course
sobremesa   dessert
sopa   soup

de hortaliça   vegetable soup
de ervas   green vegetable soup
transmontana   vegetable soup
  with bacon and bread
tâmaras   dates
tamboril   monkfish
tomates   tomatoes
toranja   grapefruit
tripas   tripe
  à moda do Porto   tripe, Oporto
  style (with beans)
truta   trout
uvas   grapes
vagens   green beans
veado   venison
vinagre   vinegar
vitela   veal

The drinks

água mineral   mineral water
água pé   light wine
aguardente   brandy
bagaço   spirit made from grape
husks
batido   milk shake
bica   small black coffee (very
strong)
branco/a   white
brandymel   honey-brandy
café   coffee
  com leite/o garoto   small
  white coffee
  descafeinado   decaffeinated
  coffee
caneca   draught beer (usually
lager)
cerveja   beer/lager
  preta   dark beer
chá   tea
  com (leite/limão)   tea with
  (milk/lemon)
  limão   lemon tea (ie infusion of
  lemon)
chocolate quente   hot chocolate
cola   cola
com gás   with gas, fizzy
com gelo   with ice
conhaque   cognac
doce   sweet

espumante   sparkling
fino   draught lager (in the north)
fresco/a   ice cold
galão   white coffee (large, milky)
gin-tónico   gin and tonic
Ginjinha   spirit distilled from
  morello cherries
imperial   draught lager
laranjada   orangeade
leite   milk
limonada   lemonade
maracujá   passion fruit juice
Moscatel   sweet dessert wine
natural   at room temperature
rosé   rosé (wine)
seco/a   dry
sem gás   without gas, still
sumo   juice
  de ananás   pineapple juice
  de fruta   fruit juice
  de laranja   orange juice
  de pêssego   peach juice
  de uva   grape juice
tinto   red wine
uísque   whisky
vinho   wine
  verde   'green' wine (see p70)
  do Porto   Port
  da Madeira   Madeira

Entertainment and leisure

Finding what's on

What is there to see here?
O que se pode ver aqui?

■ Portuguese newspapers: even a little knowledge of Portuguese will be sufficient for listings in the national and local newspaper to be useful. Those in the dailies *Público* and *Diário de Notícias* are particularly good.
■ Local tourist offices: these can supply details of local events; some even publish their own information brochures or fact sheets.
■ English-language newspapers: newsagents and kiosks in major resorts and the larger towns sell these locally produced weekly papers, such as the Algarve-based *Anglo-Portuguese News*, which usually have details of local and national events.

Spectator events

Sports

■ Football: this is the national sport, and any match is worth a visit. The season runs from around September to June, with games usually on Sundays. If you go to just one, a must is the spectacular Estádio da Luz, one of Europe's largest stadiums and home to Benfica (Lisbon, Metro Colégio Militar). Tickets for Benfica can be obtained in advance from the ticket kiosk in Lisbon's Praça dos Restauradores.
■ Bullfights: not everyone's cup of tea but the Portuguese are proud of the fact that the bullfighters can demonstrate their skills without killing the bulls in the ring. There are bullrings in many southern Portuguese towns; Cascais and Lisbon's Campo Pequeno are two of the biggest venues. Events tend to be in the evenings and Saturday afternoons from June to September. Tickets can be bought from stadium ticket offices.
■ Formula One car racing: Portugal's Grand Prix takes place in Estoril, usually in September, and there are practice runs at other times of the year.

Fairs

Portugal is proud of its culture, and most regions go to great lengths to promote traditional song and dance. These tend to be performed at local agricultural fairs and festivals, often celebrating saint's days. To catch such events, look out for details in tourist offices. (See also Holidays, festivals and events, p28.)

Do you have a plan of the town?
Tem uma planta da vila?

Music

Tourist offices can give details of classical, rock or jazz concerts and festivals. Particular to Portugal, don't miss:

■ *Fado*, Portugal's traditional folk music, can be somewhat melancholy but is often powerfully moving. Specific *fado* houses, such as those in Lisbon and Coimbra, have big-name stars, but *fado* can be most appealing when sung spontaneously by a waitress or barman in a local restaurant or café.
■ Brazilian and African music: look out for any performances of these immensely popular musical styles, the legacy of Portugal's colonial days. There are some great clubs in larger Portuguese towns which have regular live Brazilian and African bands. (See Lisbon, p4.)

Cinema

Films are nearly always shown in the original-language version with Portuguese subtitles, although the film titles may be different in translation to the English equivalent.

Where does the tour start?
Onde começa a visita?

Participation events

■ Swimming: with miles of Atlantic coastline, you are never far from a beach in Portugal. However, take great care, especially on the west coast where the sea can be fierce and currents dangerous. Most towns have a municipal swimming pool, although Portugal's official swimming season runs from June to September. Outside these months, pools are closed and the Portuguese consider the sea too cold (though foreigners may disagree)!
■ Golf: Portugal has the perfect climate for golf; there are 34 courses, most on the Algarve where there is a great concentration of courses around Vilamoura and Vale do Lobo. Further north there are also good courses, such

Vilamoura

as in Estoril, near Lisbon, and Ponte de Lima in the Minho.
■ Tennis: there are tennis courts in many towns and resorts, often as part of a hotel complex, especially in the Algarve. Municipal courts can usually be booked too, although some of them require 24 hours' notice.
■ Walking: the Portuguese are not great walkers, which means that once you are away from a road in rural areas, you are likely to be alone! Inland Portugal in particular has some superb walking country. Walking is excellent in Portugal's National Parks, especially Peneda-Gerês (the Minho), Serra da Estrela (Beira Alta) and Montesinho (Trás-os-Montes). Park offices and local tourist offices can give advice on good walking routes and camping spots.

Portugal dos Pequeninos

■ Bird watching: Portugal has some
unspoilt habitats ideal for migratory
birds and waders, especially in its
coastal estuaries and mudflats such
as at Quinta da Rocha and Rio
Formosa in the Algarve, the Tejo
nature reserve north of Lisbon, and
São Jacinto on the Aveiro lagoon in
the Beira Litoral.
■ Picnicking: this is a great
Portuguese pastime. In summer
and at weekends, most parks,
beauty spots and *miradouros*
(panoramic view points) are busy
with sprawling family groups
tucking into substantial picnics.
The drawback is that litter quickly
accumulates in popular spots.
■ Fishing and hunting: check in
tourist offices or the local *Câmara
Municipal* (town hall) for the need for
permits and equipment hire details.
Fishing is good both along the coast
(resorts such as Lagos in the Algarve
offer fishing cruises) and off Madeira,
and in Portugal's inland lakes and
rivers (such as the Minho). Hunting
is popular especially in inland areas
where game – even wild boar – is
still common.
■ Cycling and horse riding: local
tourist offices can give details of cycle
hire and horse-riding possibilities.
Horse breeding is big business in the
Alentejo and the Ribatejo regions,
while pony trekking is popular in
Gerês.
■ Surfing and skiing: surfing is a big
sport in Portugal; Guincho near
Lisbon holds international events,
while specialized surf centres such as
that in Espinho south of Oporto can
hire out equipment. Skiing is
confined to the mountainous Serra
da Estrela, based in Penhas da Saúde
during winter only.
■ Sailing: the Portuguese tourist
board publish a brochure detailing
Portugal's main sailing facilities and
marinas.

Children

Portugal is generally a safe and child-
friendly country. Some popular
attractions for children include:
Onda parks Several towns, such as
Caparica outside Lisbon, Beja in the
Alentejo and Amarante outside
Oporto, have *onda* (wave) parks, a
series of slides and pools which are
great fun for older children.
Portugal dos Pequeninos, Coimbra
(see p19).

Where can I buy tickets?
Onde compro bilhetes?

Safe beaches

Beaches can be
dangerous in Portugal,
and it is best to take care
that children do not go
out of their depth. The
south-facing Algarve is
generally safe. A selection of
Portugal's more child-friendly
beaches includes:
■ Algarve: most beaches, especially
Lagos (see p23).
■ Alentejo: Porto Covo, Lagoa de
Santo André (lagoon), Lagoa de
Malides (see p24–25).
■ Lisbon coast: Portinho da
Arrábida, Lagoa de Albufeira
(lagoon).
■ Estremadura: Foz do Arelho
(lagoon), São Martinho do Porto
(see p19).
■ Coimbra coast: Praia do
Cabedelo, Figueira da Foz (see p19).
■ Costa Verde: Praia do Cabedelo
(Viana do Castelo), Vila Praia de
Âncora (see p14).

Phrasemaker
Getting to know the place

Do you have (a plan of the town/an entertainment guide)?	**Tem (uma planta da vila/um guia de distracções)?**
Do you have any information in English?	**Tem informações em inglês?**
What is there to (see/do) here?	**O que se pode (ver/fazer) aqui?**
Is there (a guided tour/ a bus tour)?	**Há (visita guiada/visita de autocarro)?**
Are there any (cinemas/ night-clubs) here?	**Há (cinemas/boîtes) aqui?**
Can you recommend a restaurant?	**Podia recomendar um restaurante?**
Is there anything for children to do?	**Há distracções para crianças?**

Há visita guiada.	There's a guided tour.
Há dois teatros.	There are two theatres.
Em que está interessado?	What are you interested in?

Things to do or see

bullfight	**a tourada**
cinema	**o cinema**
concert	**o concerto**
dance hall	**o salão de baile**
discotheque	**a discoteca**
exhibition	**a exposição**
fiesta/celebration	**a festa**
fireworks	**os fogos de artifício**
football match	**o jogo de futebol**
funfair	**a feira**
gallery	**a galeria**
golf course	**o campo de golfe**
museum	**o museu**
night-club	**a boîte**
show	**o espectáculo**
stadium	**o estádio**
swimming pool	**a piscina**
tennis (courts/match)	**(os campos/o jogo) de ténis**
theatre	**o teatro**

Getting more information

Where is (the swimming pool/ the concert hall)?	**Onde é (a piscina/a sala de concertos)?**
Where does the tour start?	**Onde começa a visita?**
What time does it (start/finish)?	**A que horas (começa/termina)?**
When is it open?	**Quando está aberto?**
Will I need tickets?	**Preciso de bilhetes?**
Are there any tickets?	**Há bilhetes?**
Where can I buy tickets?	**Onde compro bilhetes?**

Não precisa de bilhetes.	You don't need tickets.
Lamento, está esgotado.	Sorry, it's sold out.
Na praça principal, às dez horas.	In the main square, at 10 o'clock.

(See p33 for clock times.)

na bilheteira	at the ticket office
aqui, (no mapa/na planta)	here, on the (map/plan)

Getting in

Do you have any tickets?	**Tem bilhetes?**
How much is it?	**Quanto é?**
Four tickets, please	**Quatro bilhetes, se faz favor**
for (Saturday/tomorrow)	**para (sábado/amanhã)**

(See p35 for days of the week.)

Are there any concessions?	**Há descontos?**
May I take photos?	**Posso tirar fotografias?**
How long does it last?	**Quanto tempo dura?**
Does the film have subtitles?	**O filme tem legendas?**
Is there (a programme/ an interval)?	**Há (programa/intervalo)?**
Are the seats numbered?	**Os lugares estáo numerados?**
Is this place taken?	**Este lugar está vago?**

Sim, para (estudantes/ crianças/reformados).	Yes, for (students/children/ pensioners).
um intervalo de vinte minutos	one interval of 20 minutes
Está (livre/ocupado).	It's (free/taken).

Signs

balcão	circle
bar	bar
camarote	box
casa de banho	toilets
escada	stairs
homens	gents
lavabos	toilets
mulheres	ladies
plateia	stalls
retretes	toilets
saída	exit
sanitários	toilets
senhoras	ladies
senhores	gents
vestiário	cloakroom

Swimming and sunbathing

Can I use the hotel pool?	**Posso usar a piscina do hotel?**
Where are (the changing rooms/the showers)?	**Onde são os (vestiários/ chuveiros)?**
I'd like to hire (a deck chair/ a towel).	**Queria alugar (uma cadeira de lona/uma toalha).**

On the beach

bathing hut	**a barraca**	sunbed	**a espregui-çadeira**
boat	**o barco**	sunglasses	**os óculos de sol**
life-guard	**o salva-vidas**	suntan cream	**o creme para bronzear**
life-belt	**o cinto de salvação**	table	**a mesa**
parasol	**o guardasol**		

Sports

Where can I (go swimming/ play tennis)?

Onde posso (ir nadar/jogar ténis)

I'd like to hire (a racket/ waterskis).

Queria alugar (uma raqueta/ esquis aquáticos).

I'd like to take sailing lessons.

Queria ter lições de vela.

climbing	**o alpinismo**	volleyball	**o voleibol**
football	**o futebol**	walking	**as excursóes a pé**
golf	**o golfe**	water-ski	**o esqui aquático**
riding	**a equitação**	wind-surfing	**o wind-surf**
sailing	**a vela**		
surfing	**o surf**		
tennis	**o ténis**		

Sports equipment

boots	**as botas**
dinghy/sailing boat	**o barco à vela**
golf clubs	**os tacos de golfe**
surf-board	**a prancha de surf**
tennis balls	**as bolas de ténis**
tennis racket	**a raqueta de ténis**
water-skis	**os esquis aquáticos**
wind-surf board	**a prancha à vela/a prancha de wind-surf**

4 You don't want to miss a show and try to book seats.

- **Tem bilhetes para amanhã?**
- □ **Lamento, está esgotado.**
- **Tem bilhetes para sábado?**
- □ **Sim, senhor.**

What day can you see the show?

5 You are buying tickets to see a film.

- **Quatro bilhetes, se faz favor. Há descontos?**
- □ **Sim, para crianças.**
- **Dois adultos e duas crianças. Quanto é?**
- □ **Para dois adultos, mil escudos; para duas crianças, setecentos escudos.**

(See p33 for numbers.)

What is the total cost?

Language works

Getting to know the place

You are in the tourist office.
Tem informações em inglês?
Não, senhor. Em que está interessado?
Há campos de golfe aqui?
Há dois campos de golfe.

How many golf courses are there?

Getting more information

A Portuguese friend tells you about a concert that's on.
Onde é o concerto?
É na praça principal.
A que horas?
Às sete horas.
Preciso de bilhetes?
Não precisa de bilhetes.

Will you need to get tickets in advance? Yes or no?

The hotel receptionist answers your questions about an excursion.
A que horas começa a visita?
Às dez horas.
A que horas termina?
Às sete da tarde.

How long does the excursion last?

Praia da Marina de Vilamoura

Praia vigiada
Balneários com duche quente
Parque Infantil
Diversões aquáticas
Quiosque
Restaurante Casa da Praia
Estacionamento vigiado
Sandwich Bar

Bom Dia!

Try it out

Wordsearch

Can you find the fifteen words from this chapter hidden here? Words go up and down, backwards and forwards, and diagonally.

E	S	P	E	C	T	A	C	U	L	O
S	B	H	X	N	A	L	Z	E	V	I
Q	O	C	P	G	M	E	D	S	B	R
U	L	M	O	E	J	V	A	U	C	A
I	F	E	S	T	A	I	H	M	G	I
S	R	A	I	O	D	S	L	F	O	T
D	U	K	C	A	Y	I	A	N	L	S
E	S	C	A	D	A	T	O	H	F	E
P	Q	U	O	I	D	A	T	S	E	V

Match them up!

Can you match up the following to make sensible phrases?

óculos	à vela
prancha	de golfe
raqueta	de baile
tacos	de wind-surf
salão	de sol
barco	de ténis

Scrambled words

Use these clues to help you unscramble these words:
1 All change here for the sea
   aracrab
2 This activity will get you to the top
   mainspoil
3 Picture palace
   iceman
4 Essential furniture for holiday activity!
   eriç a spare guide
5 Place where works of art are displayed
   air gale
6 None left
   goat odes
7 Now you can follow the film
   aged lens
8 Time to stretch your legs and visit the bar!
   love train
9 Downstairs seating in a theatre
   tea pail
10 Not gentlemen!
   nosc rash

As if you were there

Your apartment is in the grounds of a large hotel . . .
- (Ask if you can use the hotel pool)
□ **Sim, senhor. É trezentos escudo por dia.**
- (Say you'd like to hire a sun-lounger)
□ **São quatrocentos escudos em total. Tem toalha?**
- (Say 'yes' and ask where the showers are)
□ **Ao lado da saída, senhor.**

Sound Check

Ways of pronouncing **o**.

When **o** is stressed, or when it has an acute accent, it sounds like 'o' in 'hot':
   jogo (game) sounds like 'zho-goo'
   óculos (glasses) sounds like 'o-koo-loosh'
When it's not stressed, it sounds like 'oo' in 'food':
   discoteca (discotheque) sounds like 'dish-koo-**teh**-ker'

õ is the **nasal** sound.

Emergencies

Crime

Violent crime is rare in Portugal and in many areas you need barely worry about theft. Nevertheless, Portugal does suffer from high unemployment and drugs are more widespread than in the past, so it is best to take sensible precautions wherever you stay. Always leave valuables in a safe place such as the hotel reception, be sure to lock your car and keep bags out of sight in the boot, and keep a close eye on handbags, cameras and cash, especially in crowded areas such as on public transport, in markets and in bars. Do not leave valuables unattended in tents or on the beach.

Portugal is relatively cosmopolitan, but isolated race-related incidents do occur especially in Lisbon and Oporto.

Women travelling alone may attract unwanted male attention but are unlikely to be attacked, although it is best not to walk alone late at night in large cities.

Can you help me?
Pode ajudar-me?

Dealing with the police

If you are robbed, it is sensible not to resist. Report the incident to the nearest police station as soon as possible. For emergencies the telephone number is 115. The police are unlikely to be able to find the culprit, but make sure you get a written police report for insurance purposes.

Health

You do not need to take any precautions against specific illnesses, and food and drinking water are perfectly safe. There are snakes and wolves in parts of Portugal but you are unlikely to see them and even less likely to be harmed by them. Likewise there are no dangerous insects, although mosquitoes can be a nuisance.

The main hazard in Portugal is the sun; with cooling Atlantic breezes, the sun can feel deceptively weak, especially on the coast. Always wear suncream, and keep in the shade at midday. Many resort beaches hire out sun shades, which can also be bought cheaply from tourist shops and supermarkets.

Toilets

Public toilets can be found in most coach and train stations. They are of variable standards; sometimes you will be expected to pay a small tip to the attendant. Toilets are signed *retretes*, *lavabos*, *WC* or *casa de banho*, with *senhores/homens* (H) for men and *senhoras/mulheres* (M) for women.

Medical treatment

Is there someone here who speaks English?
Há alguém aqui que fale inglês?

Should you become ill, most towns have a pharmacy (opening hours are the same as shops) which can recommend the appropriate medicine for minor ailments. They can also point you to the nearest doctor if one is necessary; be prepared to wait some time to see one and to pay for treatment, although you should be able to claim this back from insurance. In an emergency, dial 115 and you will be taken to the nearest hospital, but be

warned that these do not have a very good reputation. If you are an EU national with form E111 (available from post offices in the United Kingdom), you are entitled to free emergency treatment.

Telephones

Public telephone boxes can be found in most Portuguese towns and villages, which accept cash or a *cartão credifone* or *credi* (phone card). Most have user instructions in several languages inside, and inter-national country codes. If you wish to make an international call, it is best to buy a *credi* card, available from post offices. Larger towns also have specific telephone centres, often attached to post offices or tourist offices, where you can pay for your call at a counter after it has been made. Public telephones can also be found in bars and cafés; hotels tend to charge a higher rate for direct calls.

Post office facilities

Post offices (*correios*) can be found in nearly any Portuguese town, and they accept *posta restante* mail (sometimes for a small fee). For stamps, look for the counter marked *selos*. (See p64 on buying stamps.)

Travellers with special needs

Disabled facilities are improving in Portugal, although far from ideal. Any Portuguese Tourist Board or local tourist office can provide a list of hotels which have wheelchair access. Details of car-hire possibilities for disabled visitors can be supplied

by ARAC in Lisbon (01 563 737). The Orange Badge symbol is recognised for disabled car parking Lisbon airport also offers a service fo wheelchair users, although advance notice is required (01 363 2044).

Useful telephone numbers

Airport information:
802060 (Lisbon); 948 2144 (Porto); 089 819882 (Faro)
Emergencies: 115 (police and medical services)
Directory enquiries: 118
Operator: 099
Automóvel Clube de Portugal:
01 356 3931 (has a reciprocal agreement with automobile clubs elsewhere in Europe for breakdown)

! I need an ambulance.
Preciso duma ambulância.

Embassies and consulates in Portugal

■ **Australia** Avenida da Liberdade 244–4, Lisbon (01 523 350).
■ **Canada** Avenida da Liberdade 144–3, Lisbon (01 347 4892); Rua Frei Lourenço de Santa Maria 1–1 Faro (Algarve consulate – 089 375
■ **Ireland** Rua da Imprensa à Estre 1–4, Lisbon (01 396 1569).
■ **New Zealand** (consulate): Rua de São Félix 1200, Lisbon (01 350 969
■ **South Africa** Avenida Luís Bívar 10, Lisbon (01 353 5041).
■ **UK** Rua São Bernardo 33, Lisbo (01 392 4000); Avenida da Boavista 3072, Oporto (consulate – 02 684 789); Largo Francisco A. Maurício 7–1, Portimão (Algarve consulate - 082 417 800).
■ **USA** Avenida das Forças Armadas, Lisbon (01 726 6600).

Phrasemaker

General phrases

Help!	**Socorro!**
Excuse me/Hello there! (to attract attention)	**Desculpe!**
Can you help me?	**Pode ajudar-me?**
Where is the (police station/hospital)?	**Onde é (a esquadra/o hospital)?**
(See p42 for directions.)	
Where is the (nearest petrol station/garage)?	**Onde é (a estação de serviço mais próxima/a garagem mais próxima)?**
Is there someone here who speaks English?	**Há alguém aqui que fale inglês?**
Thank you	**Obrigado** (said by men); **obrigada** (said by women)
Leave me alone!	**Deixe-me em paz!**
I'll call the police.	**Chamo a polícia.**

Health

I need (a doctor/an ambulance).	**Preciso (dum médico/duma ambulância).**
It's urgent.	**É urgente.**
I'd like an appointment with (a doctor/a dentist).	**Queria uma consulta com (um médico/um dentista).**
(See p33 for clock times; p35 for days of the week.)	

Parts of the body

ankle	**o tornozelo**	hip	**a anca**
arm	**o braço**	kidneys	**os rins**
back	**as costas**	knee	**o joelho**
chest	**o peito**	leg	**a perna**
chin	**o queixo**	lips	**os lábios**
ear (outer)	**a orelha**	liver	**o fígado**
ear (inner)	**o ouvido**	mouth	**a boca**
elbow	**o cotovelo**	nails	**as unhas**
eye(s)	**o(s) olho(s)**	neck	**o pescoço**
face	**a cara**	nose	**o nariz**
fingers	**os dedos**	shoulder	**o ombro**
foot	**o pé**	stomach	**o estômago**
forehead	**a testa**	thigh	**a coxa**
hand	**a mão**	throat	**a garganta**
hair	**o cabelo**	toes	**os dedos do pé**
head	**a cabeça**	tooth	**o dente**
heel	**o calcanhar**	wrist	**o pulso**

Telling the doctor

My stomach hurts	**Dói-me o estômago/ Tenho dor de estômago.**
My eyes hurt	**Doem-me os olhos.**
It hurts here.	**Dói aqui.**
(My son/ My daughter) has a temperature.	**(O meu filho/A minha filha) tem febre.**
(She/he) feels sick.	**Tem náuseas.**
Is it serious?	**E grave?**

I can't (move/feel) . . .	**Não posso (mexer/sentir) . . .**
I've been sick.	**Vomitei.**
I've got . . .	**Tenho . . .**
burns	**queimaduras**
a cold (virus)	**constipação**
constipation	**prisão de ventre**
a cough	**tosse**
diarrhoea	**diarreia**
a sore throat	**dor de garganta**
stings	**picadas**
sunburn	**insolação**
toothache	**dor de dentes**

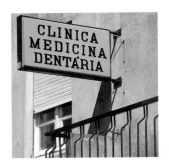

Common accidents

I've (cut/burnt) myself.	**Cortei-me/Queimei-me.**
I've been bitten by a dog.	**Fui mordido por um cão.**
I've been bitten by an insect.	**Fui picado por um insecto.**
I've lost a filling.	**Perdi um chumbo.**

Special problems

I'm allergic to (antibiotics/ animals).	**Sou alérgico/a a (antibióticos/ animais).**
I'm diabetic.	**Sou diabético/a.**
I'm pregnant.	**Estou grávida.**
I have asthma.	**Sofro de asma.**
I wear contact lenses.	**Uso lentes de contacto.**
I have toothache.	**Tenho dor de dentes.**

Qual é o problema?	What is the problem?
Há quanto tempo se sente assim?	How long have you been feeling like this?
Vou examiná-lo.	I'm going to examine you.
Dispa-se, se faz favor.	Please undress.
Deite-se ali.	Lie down there.
Onde lhe dói?	Where does it hurt?
Não é grave.	It's not serious.
O osso está partido.	The bone is broken.
É preciso fazer uma operação.	You will need an operation.
Isto é uma receita.	This is a prescription.
Vou meter-lhe um chumbo (provisório).	I'll put in a (temporary) filling.
Tenho de tirar-lhe este dente.	I'll have to take this tooth out.

At the chemist's

Do you have something for . . .?	**Tem alguma coisa para . . .?**
Do you have any . . .?	**Tem . . .?**
after-sun lotion	**a loção hidratante**
antibiotics	**os antibióticos**
anti-histamine	**a anti-histamina**
aspirin	**as aspirinas**
baby food	**a comida para bebé**
contact-lens solution	**o líquido para lentes de contacto**
contraceptives	**os contraceptivos**
cough mixture	**o xarope para a tosse**
cream	**o creme**

lotion	**a loção**
medicine	**o medicamento**
nappies	**as fraldas**
paracetamol	**o paracetamol**
pills/tablets	**os comprimidos**
plasters	**os adesivos**
sanitary towels	**os pensos higiénicos/as toalhas absorventes**
sunglasses	**os óculos de sol**
suntan cream	**o creme para bronzear**

Tome estes comprimidos . . .	Take these tablets . . .
Aplique esta loção . . .	Apply this lotion . . .
. . . (uma vez/duas vezes/ três vezes) por dia.	(once/twice/three times) a day.
. . . (antes das/depois das) refeições.	. . . (before/after) meals.
. . . com água.	. . . with water.
Mastigue, não (morda/engola).	Chew, don't (bite/swallow).
Deve (descansar/dormir).	You must (rest/sleep).
Não deve (levantar-se/ correr/fazer exercício).	You mustn't (get up/run/take exercise).

Car breakdown

I've broken down	**Tive uma avaria**
on the motorway E4	**na auto-estrada E4**
. . . 5 kilometres from . . .	**. . . a cinco quilómetros de . . .**
The (engine/steering) isn't working.	**(O motor/A direcção) não funciona.**
The brakes aren't working.	**Os travões não funcionam.**
I've got a flat tyre.	**Tenho um pneu furado.**
I've run out of petrol.	**Acabou-se-me a gasolina.**
When will it be ready?	**Quando estará pronto?**
(See p33 for clock times; p35 for days of the week.)	

Qual é o problema?
What's the problem?

Onde fica, exactamente?
Where are you exactly?

Demoramos uma hora.
We'll be with you in an hour.

Está pronto na próxima sexta.
It'll be ready next Friday.

Tenho de encomendar as peças.
I'll have to order the parts.

Car parts

accelerator	**o acelerador**		tyres	**os pneus**
brakes	**os travões**		wheels	**as rodas**
clutch	**a embraiagem**		windows	**as janelas**
radiator	**o radiador**		windscreen	**o limpia-parabrisas**
steering wheel	**o volante**		wiper	

Theft or loss

I've lost my (wallet/passport).	**Perdi (a minha carteira/o meu passaporte).**
I've had my (watch/bag) stolen.	**Roubaram-me o meu (relógio/saco).**
yesterday (morning/afternoon/evening)	**ontem (de manhã/à tarde/à noite)**
(last night/this morning)	**(ontem à noite/hoje de manhã)**
(in the street/in a store)	**(na rua/numa loja)**

Que aconteceu?	What happened?
Quando . . . ?	When . . . ?
Onde . . . ?	Where . . . ?
Qual é . . .	What is . . .
. . . o seu nome e morada?	. . . your name and address?
. . . a sua matrícula?	. . . your car registration?
. . . o número do seu passaporte?	. . . your passport number?
Preencha este impresso.	Fill in this form.
Volte mais tarde.	Come back later.

Valuables

briefcase	**a pasta**		jewellery	**as jóias**
camera	**a máquina fotográfica**		money	**o dinheiro**
			necklace	**o colar**
car	**o carro**		passport	**o passaporte**
credit cards	**os cartões de crédito**		purse	**a carteira**
			suitcase	**a mala**
driving licence	**a carta de condução**		tickets	**os bilhetes**
handbag	**o saco de mão**		wallet	**a carteira**

Language works

Getting medical help

1 Talking to a doctor
- **Dói-me o estômago.**
- □ **Deite-se ali – vou examiná-lo . . .
  Não é grave. Isto é uma receita.**

What does the doctor say?
a You will have to go to hospital.
b You haven't got anything serious.
c He doesn't know what's wrong.

At the chemist's

2 You need to sort out a worrying holiday illness.
- **Tem alguma coisa para diarreia?**
- □ **Sim, senhora. Tome estes
  comprimidos, com água, três
  vezes por dia.**
- **Antes das refeições?**
- □ **Não. Depois das refeições.**
- **Obrigada.**

How do you take the pills?
Put a tick in the correct boxes:

once a day	□
twice a day	□
three times a day	□
with water	□
without water	□
before meals	□
after meals	□

Car breakdown

3 You phone a garage for help.
- **Tive uma avaria.**
- □ **Qual é o problema?**
- **A embriagem não funciona.**
- □ **Demoramos uma hora.**

The garage will come and help you:
true/false?

Theft

4 You report a robbery at the police station.
- **Roubaram-me o meu saco.**
- □ **Quando?**
- **Hoje de manhã.**
- □ **Onde?**
- **Na rua Barata.**
- □ **Preencha este impresso, se faz
  favor.**

What have you got to do to help the police get your bag back?
a Go to the Rua Barata.
b Return to the police station the next day.
c Fill in a form.

Try it out

What's the question?

The following questions have the spaces between the words in the wrong places. See if you can rearrange them and understand what they mean.
a **Háal gue maqui quefa leing lês?**
b **On del hed ói?**
c **Temas piri nas?**
d **Quan does tárap ron to?**
e **Qua léo se uno meem or ada?**

Matching

Match up the halves of the sentences below to make sense of what you're saying!

Chamo	**o meu relógio.**
Preciso	**tosse.**
Queria	**o dedo.**
Tenho	**a polícia.**
**Não posso
mexer**	**uma consulta.**
Perdi	**duma ambulância.**

As if you were there

A visit to the dentist's.
- □ **Qual é o problema?**
- ■ (Tell the dentist you have lost a filling and have a toothache)
- □ **Vou examiná-lo. Deite-se ali . . .**
- ■ (Ask if it is serious)
- □ **Não. Vou meter-lhe um chumbo provisório.**
- ■ (Thank him)

Unravelling

Mixed-up body parts: rearrange to find a part of your body.

coax	**broom**
vote loco	**coasts**
tag a gran	

Car problems: do the same to find things to do with cars.

roads	**ant love**
alec roared	**rag game**
as in goal	

Gap fill

If you can do this you will be able to read down the middle an essential item for driving abroad.

1		OLAR
2	MAL	
3		ADIADOR
4	HOSPI	AL
5		LGUEM
6	GRÁVI	A
7		MBRAIAGEM
8	EXERCÍ	IO
9		SSO
10	PER	A
11		IABÉTICO
12	AQ	I
13		ÃO
14	ANIM	IS
15		LHOS

Clues:
1 Neck jewellery.
2 Pack it before a holiday.
3 Might belong in a house or in a car.
4 You might end up here if you have an accident.
5 Someone/anyone!
6 With child.
7 You need this to change gear.
8 Energetic movement.
9 What our skeleton is made up of.
10 Shake a . . . !
11 You probably use insulin.
12 Not there.
13 Not a cat.
14 Wildlife.
15 Use your . . . to see.

Sound check

c, **ç**, and **ch**
c followed by 'e' or 'i' and **ç** sound like 's' in 'sun'; **c** followed by anything else sounds like 'c' in 'cat':

> **cinema** sounds like 'see-**neh**-mer';
> **começa** (begins) sounds like 'koo-**meh**-ser'

ch sounds like 'sh' in 'shed':
> **chapéu** (hat) sounds like 'shar-**peh**-oo'

Language builder

The words and phrases in this book will enable you to get by in Portuguese in everyday situations, but there may come a time when you want to say a little more. This is when you need to look at how you can create your own sentences. This section shows how you how to fit together the building blocks of language: the words.

Articles: 'a' and 'the'

'a'
There are two words for 'a' in Portuguese, **um** and **uma**. You say '**um café**' but '**uma cerveja**'. This is because the words for all Portuguese things or people (nouns) are either masculine or feminine.

Um goes with masculine words and **uma** with feminine words. It is not always easy to know whether a noun is masculine or feminine, but in general if it ends in **-o** it is masculine and if it ends in **-a** it is feminine.

um castelo	(a castle)
uma loja	(a shop)
um apartamento	(an apartment)
uma camisa	(a shirt)
um banco	(a bank)
uma garrafa	(a bottle)

'the'
There are four words for 'the'. Again, the right one depends on whether the word that goes with it is masculine or feminine, but this time it also depends on whether there is just one of them (singular) or more than one (plural).

When you are referring to just one thing or person, you use **o** for masculine words or **a** for feminine ones. If there is more than one thing or person, simply add an '**s**' to the Portuguese word for 'the'.

o cinto	(the belt)
os cintos	(the belts)
a sardinha	(the sardine)
as sardinhas	(the sardines)

Singular and plural

When you are talking about more than one person or thing, you normally add an 's' to the word:

azeitonas	(olives)
cebolas	(onions)
sapatos	(shoes)

There are some exceptions to this rule, which are important because they often apply to common words:

-z: **ascensor, ascensores**
n: **jardim, jardins**
o: **galão, galões**
l, -el, -ol, -il: **postal, postais**

Adjectives

These words have different
endings, which depend on the
noun that they describe. The
noun is either masculine or
feminine, and it is also either
singular or plural. For example, if
the noun is feminine then the
adjective that you use must also
be in its feminine form. Here, the
adjective is the word for 'dirty':
sujo
um carro (a car)
  um carro sujo (a dirty car)
uma faca (a knife)
  uma faca suja (a dirty knife)
In most cases you change the 'o'
at the end of the adjective to an
'a' to make the adjective
feminine.

If the noun is masculine plural,
then the adjective also must be
in the masculine plural form.
frango (chicken)
  frango assado (roast chicken)
um pimento (a pepper)
  pimentos assados (roast
  peppers)

In general, as you can see from
the examples given, the adjective
is placed after the noun.

Talking about possession and relationships

The following words are
adjectives and so they change
according to the noun that they
describe:

my:
o meu carro (my car)
  a minha casa (my house)
os meus sapatos (my shoes)
  as minhas gambas (my prawns)
your:
o teu carro
  a tua casa
os teus sapatos
  as tuas gambas
your/his/her/their:
o seu carro
  a sua casa
os seus sapatos
  as suas gambas

our:
o nosso carro
  a nossa casa
os nossos sapatos
  as nossas gambas

This, that, these, those

Once again, the right word always
depends on whether the object
you are pointing out is masculine
or feminine, singular or plural.
This is because you are using a
type of adjective.

This, these:
este melão, estes melões
this melon, these melons
esta saia, estas saias
this skirt, these skirts
That, those:
esse melão, esses melões
that melon, those melons
essa saia, essas saias
that skirt, those skirts

Talking to people

There are a few words for 'you' in Portuguese. It depends on who you are talking to.

For example, if you are talking to a stranger it is best to be polite and say **o senhor** (to a man) or **a senhora** (to a woman). You do the same whenever you feel the need to be polite, even if you already know the person.

Once you have become friendly with someone and can be more informal you can use the word **você** (to men or women).

There is a third word, **tu**, which you should only use for very informal friendships. Families use it among themselves, and so do close friends.

Verbs

Verbs, which are the words that express actions, change their endings frequently – far more than in English. What makes them change their endings is the person who is doing the action. There are five possible endings for every verb in Portuguese:

falo	I speak
falas	you speak (very informal only)
fala	you speak; he/she speaks
falamos	we speak
falam	you (plural) speak; they speak

This is the pattern for most verbs. The example given is for **falar** (to speak), which is a typical **-ar** verb.

There are two other common patterns of verbs: those which end in **-er** and those which end in **-ir**. The table below shows the endings of typical verbs of these types.

comer to eat:

como	I eat
comes	you eat (very informal)
come	you eat; he/she eats
comemos	we eat
comem	you (plural) eat; they eat

abrir to open:

abro	I open
abres	you open (very informal)
abre	you open; he/she opens
abrimos	we open
abrem	you (plural) open; they open

Pronouns

You can see from the verbs above that the words for 'I', 'you' 'he', 'she', 'we' and 'they' are not generally used in Portuguese

...hey do exist, but the only time
...ou will really need them is when
...ou need to say the right word for
...'you': **o senhor**, **a senhora**, **você**
...nd **tu**.
...f you are having difficulty in
...making yourself understood, you
...may wish to use the pronouns to
...make it clear. Here is the full list:

	eu
...ou (very informal)	**tu**
...ou (quite friendly)	**você**
...ou (polite)	**o senhor/ a senhora**
...e	**ele**
...he	**ela**
...e	**nós**
...ou (plural, quite friendly)	**vocês**
...ou (plural, polite)	**os senhores/ as senhoras**
...ey	**eles/elas**

...he verb 'to be'

...here are three quite different
...erbs that express 'am', 'is' and
...are': they are called
...**er**, **estar** and **ficar**. (There is a
...ourth way of saying 'is' or 'are' –
...**á** – which means 'there is' or
...here are'.)

...**água está fria!**
...he water is cold!
...**nde estão os meus sapatos?**
...here are my shoes?
...these two examples you use
...**star** because you are talking
...bout states that can change
...ou were perhaps hoping the
...ater was warm; and the shoes
...e not where you expected them
... be).

...**ão americanos.**
...ey are American.
...**nde é a igreja?**
...here is the church?
...ere you use **ser** because you

are talking about a permanent
quality (the fact that they are
American), and a fixed location.

Onde fica a igreja?
Where is the church?
Fica longe?
Is it far?
When talking about location you
can use **ficar**.

Questions

This is not difficult – you simply
say what you want in a
questioning way! For example,
'You have free rooms' is **Tem
quartos vagos**. If you want to ask
if they have any free rooms, you
say **Tem quartos vagos?** In other
words you do not have to change
the word order. Instead, you
should make your voice rise in
pitch at the end of the question,
just as you normally do in your
own language.
You may often want to ask
specific questions with words
like 'when', 'where' and 'how'.
Here is a short list of these
words:

Where . . .?	**Onde . . .?**
When . . .?	**Quando . . .?**
How . . .?	**Como . . .?**
Who . . .?	**Quem . . .?**
Why . . .?	**Porque . . .?**
What . . .?	**Que . . .?**
How much . . .?	**Quanto . . .?**
Which . . .?	**Qual . . .?**

Answers

Bare necessities
1 tomorrow; 2 afternoon; 50 escudos; 3 4,800 escudos

The numbers game
seis, cinco, três, dois, trinta, trezentos, dez mil, dois mil

Where are we now?
a Irlanda, Portugal; b Espanha; c Itália; d Alemanha; e Canadá; f Brasil; g Inglaterra, França; h Estados Unidos

Times
a São sete e meia; b São dez e um quarto; c São oito e vinte (vinte e vinte); d São três e dez (quinze e dez).

As if you were there
■ Desculpe! Bom dia.
■ Onde é o banco?
■ A que horas fecha?
■ Obrigado/a.
■ Adeus.

Getting around
1 second left; 2 false; 3 7 o'clock; 4 yes

Wordsearch
hidroplano, bicicleta, camioneta, barco, comboio, taxi, carro, avião, autocarro, metro

Locations
banco, castelo, praia, museu, estação, praça, largo

Somewhere to stay
1 how many nights you'll be staying; 2 8,000 escudos; 3 value-added tax; 4 false; 5 11 am; 6 false; 7 12,000 escudos; 8 2,000 escudos

Matching
1d, 2a, 3b, 4e, 5c

Crossword
Across: 5 televisão; 6 cama; 7 janela; 9 zero
Down: 1 duche; 2 carro; 3 piscina; 4 tenda; 6 cofre; 8 luz

As if you were there
■ Queria pagar a conta.
■ (Número) Oito.
■ Quanto é?
■ Em dinheiro.

Jumbled words
1c elevador; 2e adultos; 3d problema; 4a noite; 5b passaporte

Buying things
1 there are several kinds; 2 yes; 3 120 escudos; 4 it is very expensive; 5 left

Shopping list
1 lata/sardinhas; 2 gramas/queijo; 3 garrafa/mineral; 4 quilo/presunto 5 litro/vinho

Crossword
Across: 1 sapato; 2 camisa
Down: 1, 5 across and 3 down saco de mão; 4 saia

As if you were there
■ Queria provar sapatos.
■ O meu número inglês é seis.
■ Preto.
■ Fico com eles.

Opposites: 1 pequeno (small); 2 largo (wide/broad); 3 caro (expensive).

Café life
1 no; 2 what you want to drink; 3 no, there are steak sandwiches too; 4 420 escudos; 5 vanilla

Find the word:
1 sumo de fruta; 2 refrigerantes; 3 gelado; 4 batido; 5 tosta; 6 garot 7 prego; 8 morango; 9 sandes

112

As if you were there
■ Faz favor! Queria um gin-tónico.
■ Sim. E um vinho branco.
  Queria provar acepipes variados.

Downword
1 baunihla; 2 troco; 3 temos; 4 sem;
5 rissóis; 6 tonico; 7 sabores;
8 batatas fritas

Eating out
1 10; 2 true; 3 chicken, wine;
4 true; 5 dry; 6 near the door;
7 2,200 escudos

Crossword
Across: 4 guardanapo; 5 faca;
9 cerveja
Down: 1 vinho; 2 copo; 3 sal;
4 garfo; 6 colher; 7 pimenta;
8 prato

Matching halves
MESA, LULAS, PORTA, MOLHO,
CARNE, SOPA.

The right course

Food	Menu heading
BORREGO	CARNE
ERVILHAS	LEGUMES
AZEITONAS	ACEPIPES
FRANGO	AVES
AMBAS	MARISCOS

Entertainment and leisure
1 two golf courses; 2 no; 3 9 hours;
4 Saturday; 5 1,700 escudos

Wordsearch
spectáculo, esquis, surf, exposição,
estiário, estádio, golfe, museu, vela,
esta, visita, toalha, escada, mesa,
saída.

Match them up!
óculos de sol, prancha de wind-surf,
raqueta de ténis, tacos de golfe, salão
de baile, barco à vela

Scrambled words
1 barraca; 2 alpinismo; 3 cinema;

4 espreguiçadeira; 5 galeria;
6 esgotado; 7 legendas; 8 intervalo;
9 plateia; 10 senhoras

As if you were there
■ Posso usar a piscina do hotel?
■ Queria alugar uma espreguiçadeira.
■ Sim. Onde são os chuveiros?

Emergencies
1b; 2 three times a day, with water,
after meals; 3 true; 4 fill in a form

What's the question?
a Há alguém aqui que fale inglês?
  (Is there someone here who
  speaks English?)
b Onde lhe dói?
  (Where does it hurt?)
c Tem aspirinas?
  (Do you have any aspirin?)
d Quando estará pronto?
  (When will it be ready?)
e Qual é o seu nome e morada?
  (What is your name and address?)

Matching
Chamo a polícia; Preciso duma
ambulância; Queria uma consulta;
Tenho tosse; Não posso mexer o
dedo; Perdi o meu relógio.

As if you were there
■ Perdi um chumbo. Tenho dor de
  dentes.
■ É grave?
■ Obrigado.

Unravelling
coxa, ombro, cotovelo, costas,
garganta
rodas, volante, acelerador, garagem,
gasolina

Gap fill
1 colar; 2 mala; 3 radiador;
4 hospital; 5 alguem; 6 grávida;
7 embriagem; 8 exercício; 9 osso;
10 perna; 11 diabético; 12 aqui;
13 cão; 14 animais; 15 olhos;
16 carta de condução

Dictionary

(see also Menu reader, p85)

a to
a, as the (f)
a pé on foot, walking
aberto/a open
abrir to open
acabar to finish
aceitar to accept
acelerador, o accelerator
acender to light up
acepipes variados, os hors d'œuvres
acontecer to happen
acordar to wake up
açucar, o sugar
adaptador, o adaptor
adesivos, os plasters
adeus good bye
adulto, o adult
agora now
água, a water
água mineral, a mineral water
aguardente, o brandy
aí there
ainda não not yet
ajudar to help
albergaria, a inn
alérgico/a allergic
alface, a lettuce
alfândega, a customs
alguém somebody
alguma coisa something
alho, o garlic
almofada, a pillow
alperce, o apricot
alpinismo, o climbing
alugado/a hired, rented
alugar to hire
amanhã tomorrow
amarelo/a yellow
ambulância, a ambulance
ameixa, a plum
amêndoa, a almond
amendoin, o peanut
ananás, o pineapple
anca, a hip

andar, o floor, storey
antes de before
antibióticos, os antibiotics
antiquário, o antique shop
ao lado de next to, beside
ao pé de next to
apartamento, o flat, apartment
aperitivo, o aperitif
aplicar to apply, put on
aquele/a that
aqui here
ar, o air
ar condicionado, o air conditioning
artigo, o article
artigos de verga, os wickerwork
ascensor, o lift
aspirinas, as aspirins
assim like this, thus
assinar to sign
até a until/as far as
atrás behind
atravessar to cross
auto-estrada, a motorway
autocarro, o bus
avaria, a breakdown (of car)
avelã, a hazelnut
avião, o plane
avisar to inform, advise
azeite, o oil
azeitonas, as olives
azul blue
azulejo, o tile

bacalhau, o cod
bagagem, a luggage
balcão, o circle (in theatre)
banana, a banana
banco, o bank
barato/a cheap
barco, o boat
barco à vela, o dinghy/sailing boat
barraca, a bathing hut
bastante quite, fairly
batata, a potato
batatas fritas, as chips
batido, o milk shake
baunilha, a vanilla
bebê, o baby
beber to drink

ebida, a drink
em well
erinjela, a aubergine
ica, a black coffee (very strong)
icicleta, a bike
ifana, a pork roll
ife, o steak
ilhete, o ticket
ilhete de ida e volta, o
return ticket
ilhete turístico, o tourist
pass/ticket
ilheteira, a ticket office
lusa, a blouse
oa noite good night
oa tarde good
afternoon/evening
oca, a mouth
ocado, o bit
oîte, a night-club
olas de ténis, as tennis balls
olinhos de amêndoa, os almond
biscuits
olo, o cake
olsa, a bag
olsa de mão, a handbag
om apetite! enjoy your meal!
om, boa good
om dia good morning
ordados, os embroidery
otas, as boots
raço, o arm
ranco/a white
ronzear to sunbathe
uscar to look for

abeça, a head
abedal, o wealth
abeleireiro, o hairdresser's
abelo, o hair
achecol, o scarf
achorro (quente), o hot dog
adeira, a chair
adeira de lona, a deck
chair/lounger
aderneta, a booklet of tickets
afé, o café (for a larger range of
snacks)/coffee
afeína, a caffeine
ais, o platform
aixa, a till, cash desk

caixa forte, a deposit box
caixote de lixo, o dustbin
calcanhar, o heel
calças, as trousers
calções, os shorts
cama, a bed
camarões, os shrimps
camarote, o box (in theatre)
câmbio, o exchange (rate)
caminho, o way, road
caminho de ferro, o railway
camioneta, a coach
camisa, a shirt
camisola, a sweater
campo de golfe, o golf course
campo de ténis, o tennis court
caneta, a pen
cão, o dog
cara, a face
caravana, a caravan
carne, a meat
carnes frias, as cold meat
caro/a expensive, dear
carro, o car
carta, a letter
carta de condução, a driving
licence
cartão, o card, pass
cartão de crédito, o credit card
cartão de telefone, o telephone
card
carteira, a wallet/purse
casa de banho, a toilet, bathroom
casa de fados, a restaurant where
you will hear the traditional
Portuguese fado music
casa de hóspede, a hostel
casaco, o jacket
casal, o (married) couple
castanha, a chestnut
castanho/a brown
castelo, o castle
cataplana, a type of cooking pot
catedral, a cathedral
cebola, a onion
cem hundred (see p33)
cenoura, a carrot
cento hundred (see p33)
centro, o centre
centro comercial, o shopping
centre

cereja, a cherry
certo/a correct
cerveja, a beer/lager
cervejaria, a large café serving beer and shellfish
chá, o tea
chamada, a call
chamo-me my name is
chamar-se to be called
chapéu de sol, o parasol
chapéu, o hat
chave, a key
chávena, a cup
chegada, a arrival
chegar to arrive
cheio/a full
chouriço, o spicy red sausage
chumbo, o filling (at dentist's)
churrasqueira, a large café specializing in grilled or barbecue food
chuveiro, o shower
cidade, a city/town
cigarro, o cigarette
cinema, o cinema
cinto de salvação, o life-belt, life-ring
cinto, o belt
cinzeiro, o ashtray
cinzento/a grey
claro/a light (-coloured)
classe, a class
cobertor, o blanket
cobrar to charge, collect
cofre, o safe
cogumelo, o mushroom
colar, o necklace
colher, a spoon
colher de chá, o teaspoon
colherzinha, a teaspoon
collant, o tights
com with
com gás fizzy (mineral water)
com licença excuse me
comboio, o train
começar to begin
comer to eat
comerciante de vinhos, o wine merchant's
comida, a food
comissão, a commission

como how
como disse? pardon?
compostar to stamp (ticket)
comprar to buy
compreender to understand
comprimidos, os pills, tablets
concerto, o concert
confeitaria, a café for cakes and pastries
conhaque, o cognac
conhecer to know (a person or place)
constipação, a cold
consulta, a appointment (with doctor, dentist)
conta, a bill
conter to contain
conto, o one thousand escudos
contraceptivos, os contraceptives
contrôlo, o control
copo, o glass
cor, a colour
cor-de-laranja orange
cor-de-rosa pink
correio, o post office, post
correr to run
cortar to cut
cortina, a curtain
costas, as back
cotovelo, o elbow
couro, o leather
couve portuguesa, a kale
couve-flor, a cauliflower
coxa, a thigh
creio I think
creme para bronzear, o suntan cream
creme, o cream
crer to think
criança, a child
cuecas, as underpants
custar to cost

daqui a uma hora in one hour
dar to give
de from/of
dedos do pé, os toes
dedos, os fingers
deitar-se to lie down
deixar to leave

demorar to delay
dente, o tooth
dentista, o/a dentist
depois next, later
depois de after
depósito de bagagens, o left luggage
descafeinado decaffeinated
descansar to rest
descer to get off, go down
desconto, o discount
desculpe excuse me! (to attract attention)/sorry
desejar to desire, want
desodorizante, o deodorant
despir to undress
destino, o destination
desvio, o diversion
detergente para a louça, o washing-up liquid
devagar slowly
dever to have to, must
dia, o day
diabético/a diabetic
diarreia, a diarrhoea
dias úteis, os weekdays
dinheiro, o money
direcção, a steering/address
directo/a direct
direita, a right
discoteca, a discotheque
dispa-se get undressed
distracções, as distractions, entertainment
dizer to say, tell
do, da of the (singular)
doce sweet
doem (they) hurt
dói (it) hurts
dor, a pain
dormida, a room to let
dormir to sleep
dos, das of the (plural)
dose, a portion
duas vezes twice, two times
duche, o shower
durar to last

é (it, he, she) is/(you) are
ela her, it/she
ele him, it/he

eléctrico, o tram
elevador, o funicular/lift
em in
em baixo downstairs
em cima upstairs
em frente opposite
embraiagem, a clutch
ementa, a menu
encher to fill
encomendar to order
encontrar to find
endereço, o address
enfermeiro/a, o/a nurse
enganar-se to make a mistake
engolir to swallow
entrada, a entrance
equitação, a horse-riding
escada, a stairs
escola, a school
escova de dentes, a toothbrush
escuro/a dark
esgotado/a sold out
espargos, os asparagus
especialidade, a speciality
espectáculo, o show
esperar to wait (for)
espreguiçadeira, a sunbed, lounger
esquerda, a left
esquadra de polícia, a police station
esqui aquático, o waterskiing/waterski
esquina, a corner
estação, a station
estacionamento, o parking
estacionar to park
estádio, o stadium
estalagem, a inn
estar to be (see p110)
este, o east
este/a this
estes/as these
estômago, o stomach
estore, o blind (for window)
estrada, a road
estreito/a narrow
estudante, o/a student
exactamente exactly
examinar to examine
excursão, a excursion, trip

exercício, o exercise
experimentar to try (on)
exposição, a exhibition

faca, a knife
falar to speak
família, a family
farinha, a flour
farmácia, a chemist's
faróis, os headlights
fatia, a slice
fato de banho, o swimming costume
fato de treino, o tracksuit
favas, as broad beans
fazer to do, make
febre, a fever
fechado/a closed
fechar to close
feijões verdes green beans
feira, a market/funfair
férias, as holidays
ferro, o iron
ferry-boat, o ferry
festa, a fiesta/celebration/party
fiambre, o ham
ficar to be (situated)/remain
ficha, a form
fígado, o liver
figo, o fig
filha, a daughter
filho, o son
filigranas, as filigree jewellery
filme, o film
fim, o end
florista, a florist's
fogos de artifício, os fireworks
fora outside
fósforos, os matches
fotografia, a photograph
fraldas, as nappies
framboesa, a raspberry
frasco, o jar
fresco/a ice cold/cool
frio/a cold
fronha, a pillow case
fumador, o smoker
fumar to smoke
funcionar to work, function
fundo, o back, background
futebol, o football

galão, o white coffee (large, milky)
galeria de arte, a art gallery
galo de Barcelos, o the Barcelos cock
gamba, a prawn
garagem, a garage
garfo, o fork
garganta, a throat
garoto, o white coffee
garrafa, a bottle
gasóleo, o diesel
gasolina, a petrol
gelo, o ice
gin-tónico, o gin and tonic
ginásio, o fitness centre, gym
golfe, o golf
gostar de to like
gosto dele/a I like it, him/her
gosto deles/as I like them
grama, o gram
grande large
grande armazém, o department store
grãos, os chick peas
gravata, a tie
grave serious
grávida pregnant
grelhado/a grilled
guarda-sol, o parasol
guardanapo, o napkin
guardar to keep
guia, o guidebook
guiado/a guided

há there is/are
hidroplano, o hydrofoil
hoje today
homem, o man
hospedaria, a hostel

igreja, a church
imperial, a draught beer
impermeável, o raincoat
impresso, o form
incluído/a included
incluir to include
informações, as information
insecto, o insect
insolação, a sunburn, sunstroke

interessado/a interested
intervalo, o interval
ir to go
isso that (neutral)
isto this (neutral)
IVA, o VAT

janela, a window
jardim, o garden
jarro, o jug, carafe
joalharia, a jeweller's
joelho, o knee
jogar to play (sport)
jogo, o game, match
jóias, as jewellery
jornal, o newspaper

lá there
lábios, os lips
lamento I'm sorry
lâminas de barbear, as razor blades
lâmpada, a lamp
lápis, o pencil
laranja, a orange
laranjada, a orangeade
largo, o square
largo/a wide, broad
lata, a tin, can
lavabos, os toilets
lavandaria (a seco), a laundry (dry cleaner's)
lavatório, o washbasin
legendas, as subtitles
leitaria, a dairy
leite, o milk
lenços, os handkerchiefs
lenços de papel, os tissues
lentes de contacto, as contact lenses
lentilhas, as lentils
levantar-se to get up
leve light
libra esterlina, a pound sterling
lição, a lesson
licença, com excuse me
ligação, a connection
ligação exterior, a outside call (telephone)
limão, o lemon
limonada, a lemonade

limpa-parabrisas, o windscreen wiper
linha, a line, track, platform
líquido, o liquid
lista, a list
livraria, a bookseller's
livre free, available
loção, a lotion
loção hidratante, a after-sun lotion
loja, a shop
loja de artigos desportivos, a sports shop
loja de artigos fotográficos, a camera shop
loja de brinquedos, a toy shop
loja de ferragens, a hardware store
loja de lembranças, a souvenir shop
loja de produtos dietéticos, a health food shop
loja de roupas, a clothes shop
longe far
louças de barro, as earthenware
louças de porcelana, as china
lugar, o place, site
lula, a squid
luvas, as gloves

maçã, a apple
madeira, a wood
maior bigger
mais more
mais alguma coisa? anything else?
mais tarde later
mal passado underdone (meat)
mala, a suitcase
mandar to send
mandei reservar I have a reservation
mantenha-se keep, stay
mão, a hand
mapa, o map
máquina fotográfica, a camera
marcar to dial
mariscos, os shellfish, seafood
marisqueira, a shellfish and seafood restaurant
mastigar to chew

matrícula, a registration number (of car)
medicamento, o medicine
médico/a, o/a doctor
médio/a medium
meia pensão half board
meio/a half
mel, o honey
melancia, a watermelon
melão, o melon
mercado, o market
mercearia, a food shop/grocer's
mesa, a table
mesquita, a mosque
meter to put (in)
metro, o underground/metre
meu, o my
mexer to move
minha, a my
moda, a fashion
molho, o sauce
morada, a address
morango, o strawberry
morder to bite
motocicleta, a motorbike
motor, o engine (of car)
mudar to change
muito very
muito prazer nice to meet you
muito/a/os/as much/many
mulher, a woman
museu, o museum

nada nothing
nadar to swim
não no, not
não tem de quê you're welcome
nariz, o nose
natural room temperature
náuseas, as nausea
negócios, os business
no, na in the (singular)
noite, a night
logo then, next
nome, o name
norte, o north
nos, nas in the (plural)
nozes, as walnuts
numerado/a numbered
número, o number, size

o, os the (m)
obliterar to punch (ticket)
obras, as road works
obrigado/a thank you
oculista, o optician
óculos de sol, os sunglasses
ocupado/a occupied, taken
oeste, o west
olá! hello!
óleo, o oil
olhar to look
olho, o eye
ombro, o shoulder
onde where
ontem yesterday
operação, a operation
orelha, a (outer) ear
osso, o bone
ouvido, o (inner) ear
ovo estrelado, o fried egg

pacote, o packet
padaria, a bread shop
pãezinho, o bread roll
pagar to pay (for)
palitos, os toothpicks
pão, o bread
papel, o paper
papel higiénico, o toilet paper
papelaria, a stationer's
papo-secos, os bread rolls
para for, towards
paragem, a stop
parar to stop
parque, o park
parque de campismo, o campsite
parque de estacionamento, o car park
partida, a departure
partido/a broken
partir to depart
passadeira (de calças), a trouser press
passaporte, o passport
pasta, a briefcase
pasta de dentes, a toothpaste
pastéis de Belém/nata, os custard pies
pastelaria, a café or shop for cakes and pastries
paz, a peace

é, o foot
eagem, a toll
eça, a part (of car)
edir to order, ask for
eito, o chest
eixaria, a fishmonger's
eixe, o fish
ele, a leather/skin
ensão, a guest house
ensão completa full board
ensar to think
ensos higiénicos, os sanitary
owels
ente, o comb
eões, os pedestrians
equeno/a small
equeno almoço, o breakfast
êra, a pear
erder to lose
erdidos e achados lost property
erigo, o danger
ermitido allowed
erna, a leg
erto near
erto daqui near here
escoço, o neck
êssego, o peach
essoa, a person
etiscos, os titbits, snacks
eúgas, as socks
icada, a sting
icar to sting
ilha, a battery
imenta, a pepper (seasoning)
imento, o pepper (capsicum)
ires, o saucer
iscina, a swimming pool
istacho, o pistachio
lanta, a map, plan (of town)
lateia, a stalls (in theatre)
neu, o tyre
neu furado, o flat tyre
oder to be able, can
olícia, a police
onte, a bridge
or for/by/per/along
or quanto tempo for how long
orta, a door, gate
ortagem, a toll
ortão, o gate
orto, o port

português/esa Portuguese
posso I can
postal, o postcard
posto de turismo, o Tourist Office
pousada, a up-market hotel
pousada da juventude, a youth
hostel
praça, a square, market
praça de táxis, a taxi rank
praia, a beach
prancha à vela, a wind-surf board
prancha de surf, a surf-board
prancha de wind-surf, a wind-surf
board
prato, o plate, dish/course
pré-pagamento payment in
advance
precisar de to need
preço, o price
preencher to fill in
prego, o steak sandwich
presunto, o ham
preto/a black
primeiro/a first
prioridade, a priority
prisão de ventre, a constipation
problema, o problem
programa, o programme
proibido forbidden
pronto ready
provador, o fitting room
provar to try (on)
provisório/a temporary
próximo/a next
pulôver, o pullover
pulso, o wrist
púrpura purple
puxador, o handle

quando when
quanto how much
quarto, o room/quarter
quarto duplo, o double room
quarto individual, o single room
que what
que horas são? what time is it?
queijada, a cheesecake/cheese
tart
queijo, o cheese
queimadura, a burn
queimar to burn

queixo, o chin
quem who, whom
quente hot
querer to wish, want
queria I'd like
quilo, o kilo
quilómetro, o kilometre
quiosque de jornais, o news-stand

radiador, o radiator
rádio, o radio
raqueta, a racket
rebuçados, os sweets
receita, a prescription
recheado/a stuffed
recibo, o receipt
recomendar to recommend
reduzir to reduce
refeição, a meal
reformado/a retired
refrigerante, o soft drink
região, a region
regressar to return
relógio, o watch
rendas, as lacework
repetir to repeat
rés-do-chão, o ground floor
reservado/a reserved
reservar to reserve
residencial, o hotel
restaurante, o restaurant
retrete, o toilet
revelar to develop (film)
revista, a magazine
rins, os kidneys
rissóis, os fried pasties
roda, a wheel
rolo, o roll (of film)
roubar to steal, rob
roupa, a clothes
rua, a street

saber to know
sabonete, o soap
sabor, o flavour
saché, o sachet
saco, o bag
saco de mão, o handbag
saia, a skirt
saída, a exit
sal, o salt

sala de concertos, a concert hall
sala de espera, a waiting room
sala de reunião, a meeting room
salada, a salad
salão de baile, o dance hall
salão de chá, o tea room
salsa, a parsley
salva-vidas, o/a life-guard
sandálias, as sandals
sanitários, os toilets
são (they, you) are
sapataria, a shoe shop
sapatos, os shoes
sardinhas, as sardines
sauna, a sauna
se faz favor please
secador de cabelo, o hair dryer
secção, a section, department
seco/a dry
segundo/a second
segurança, a security
seguro, o insurance
sei I know
selo, o stamp
sem without
sem chumbo unleaded
sem gás still (mineral water)
sem saída no through road
semana, a week
sempre always
sempre em frente straight on
senhor, o you (m, very formal)/man, gentleman
senhora, a you (f, very formal)/woman, lady
sentar-se to sit down
sentido proibido no access
sentir to feel
ser to be (see p110)
serviço, o service
seu, o your/his/her/its
sim yes
simples single/simple
sinal, o deposit
só only
sobremesa, a pudding, dessert
socorro! help!
sofrer to suffer
sou I am
soutien, o bra
sujo/a dirty

sul, o south
sumo de fruta, o fruit juice
super, o four-star (petrol)
supermercado, o supermarket
suplemento, o supplement
surf, o surfing

T-shirt, a T-shirt
tabacaria, a tobacconist's
tacos de golfe, os golf clubs
talho, o butcher's
tâmaras, as dates
tanto faz it doesn't matter
tapete, o rug
tarde late
tarde, a afternoon/evening
tasca, a tavern
teatro, o theatre
telefone, o telephone
televisão, a television
tem (you) have/(he/she/it) has
temos (we) have
templo, o temple
tenda, a tent
tenho I have
ténis, o tennis
ter to have
terminar to end, finish
terraço, o terrace
testa, a forehead
tigela, a bowl
tipo, o type
tirar to pull out, take out
tirar fotografias to take photos
toalha, a towel
toalha de mesa, a tablecloth
toalhas absorventes, as sanitary towels
tomada, a plug (socket)
tomar to take, have
tomate, o tomato
toranja, a grapefruit
torneira, a tap
tornozelo, o ankle
torrada, a piece of toast
tosse, a cough
tosta, a toasted sandwich
tosta mista, a toasted cheese and ham sandwich
tourada, a bullfight
travões, os brakes

trazer to bring
trocar to change
troco, o change
tudo all, everything

uísque, o whisky
um pouco a little (ie not much)
uma vez once, one time
unhas, as nails
uns, umas some
urgente urgent
usar to use
uvas, as grapes

vagens, as green beans
vago/a free, unoccupied
vai (he, she) goes/(you) go
varanda, a balcony
vários/as several
vegetariano/a vegetarian
vela, a sailing/sail
velocidade, a speed
ver to see
verde green
vermelho/a red
vestiário, o cloakroom
vestido, o dress
vila, a town
vinagre, o vinegar
vinho, o wine
vinho do Porto, o port
vinho tinto, o red wine
virar to turn
visita, a visit
vista, a view
você you (fairly polite, see p111)
volante, o steering wheel
voleibol, o volleyball
voltar to return
vomitar to vomit
vôo, o flight
vou I go, am going

wind-surf, o wind-surfing

xaile, o shawl
xarope para a tosse, o cough mixture

zona, a zone, area
zona comercial, a shopping area

Titles available

For a complete languages catalogue please contact:
BBC Books, Book Service By Post,
PO Box 29,
Douglas,
Isle of Man, IM99 1BQ,
tel: 01624-675137, fax: 01624-70923

BBC books are available at all good bookshops or direct
from the publishers as above.